Englisch für Fortgeschrittene

Telekolleg II

Units 27–39

Dieter Buttjes
Paul J. Dine
Lothar Humburg

TR-Verlagsunion

TELEKOLLEG II

wird im Medienverbund von den *Kultusministerien* der Bundesländer Baden-Württemberg, Bayern, Nordrhein-Westfalen, Rheinland-Pfalz und Saarland (in Nordrhein-Westfalen und im Saarland in Zusammenarbeit mit den Einrichtungen der Weiterbildung) sowie den *Rundfunkanstalten* Bayerischer Rundfunk, Südwestfunk (für den Sendebereich Südwest 3) und Westdeutscher Rundfunk durchgeführt.

Dieser Band enthält das Arbeitsmaterial zu den 1986/87 vom Westdeutschen Rundfunk produzierten Lehrsendungen Telekolleg II/Englisch 27–39.

Zu diesem Sprachkurs ist eine Audio-Cassette erhältlich, auf der einige ausgewählte Texte des Begleitbuches wiedergegeben werden. Die betreffenden Texte sind im Buch mit dem Symbol ⚬⚬ gekennzeichnet.

Bildnachweis

Klaus Esefeld, Köln: S. 59, 73
Linda Goodwin-Huber-Wilhelm, Freising b. München: S. 10, 14, 23, 37, 46, 50, 77, 83, 103, 107, 111, 115, 124
Hartmuth Huber, München: S. 55, 121 (grafische Gestaltung)
Lothar Humburg, Köln: S. 19, 32, 68, 93, 97
WDR/Joachim Pfaff, Köln: S. 8
Woodmansterne Limited Watford: S. 87

2. unveränderte Auflage 1987
© 1987 by TR-Verlagsunion GmbH, München
Alle Rechte vorbehalten.
Umschlagfoto: Raimund M. Maxsein, München
Umschlaggestaltung: Beate C. Eberle, München
Gesamtherstellung: Druckerei Bremberger, München
ISBN 3-8058-1935-8

Contents

Vorwort	4
Some notes on British flags and on the introductory music of this course	8
Unit 27　Dover and the Garden of England *(Paul Dine)*	10
Unit 28　Markets in London *(Paul Dine)*	19
Unit 29　The British press. Sports *(Dieter Buttjes)*	28
Unit 30　Schools – old and new. The Open University *(Dieter Buttjes)*	37
Unit 31　Birmingham and its multi-racial society *(Dieter Buttjes)*	46
Unit 32　Nuclear power and an old forest *(Dieter Buttjes)*	55
Unit 33　Wales and the Welsh *(Lothar Humburg)*	64
Unit 34　Two Northern Irish towns *(Paul Dine)*	73
Unit 35　Working towards reconciliation *(Paul Dine)*	83
Unit 36　New enterprises in Scotland *(Lothar Humburg)*	93
Unit 37　The Athens of the North. Britons by the Sea *(Lothar Humburg)*	103
Unit 38　Fishermen and farmers *(Lothar Humburg)*	111
Unit 39　Borders we have crossed. People we have met *(Lothar Humburg)*	121
Answers to questions. Solutions to exercises	128
Wordlist	146

VORWORT

Liebe Telekollegiaten,

das erste Trimester unseres Englischkurses hat Ihnen Gelegenheit gegeben, Ihre fremdsprachlichen Grundkenntnisse aufzufrischen, die Sie aus der Schule oder aus dem Telekolleg I mitbrachten. In den beiden folgenden Trimestern haben Sie Ihren Wortschatz erweitern, größere Sicherheit in der Satzbildung erwerben und viele neue Redewendungen hinzulernen können. Aber Sie haben es bis jetzt nur mit „gefiltertem" Englisch zu tun gehabt. Die Autoren der Sendungen und Begleitbücher haben sich bemüht, Ihnen Texte zu bieten, die Ihrem Kenntnisstand angemessen waren. Sie sind bei der Entwicklung der grammatischen Strukturen schrittweise vorgegangen und haben darauf geachtet, daß Ihnen je *unit* nicht zu viele neue Vokabeln und idiomatische Wendungen zugemutet wurden. Auch die Moderatoren und Schauspieler in den Sendungen haben Ihnen stets nur ein besonders klar gesprochenes Englisch ohne mundartliche Einfärbung geboten.

Nun lernen Sie Englisch aber sicherlich nicht – jedenfalls nicht *nur* –, um Prüfungen zu bestehen, sondern vor allem, weil Sie sich mit Sprechern der englischen Sprache beruflich wie privat verständigen, englischen Hörfunk- und Fernsehprogrammen folgen und vielleicht auch englische Zeitungen, Fachzeitschriften oder Bücher lesen möchten. Wenn Sie hin und wieder schon einmal versucht haben, in eine englische Radiosendung hineinzuhorchen oder sich mit Reisenden aus dem *United Kingdom*, Nordamerika usw. zu unterhalten, dann werden Sie gemerkt haben, daß sich – selbst in den Medien – längst nicht alle Englischsprecher an die Regeln des „Schulenglisch" halten: viele Briten (von Iren, Amerikanern, Australiern, Indern, Afrikanern gar nicht zu reden) sprechen mit dialektalen Einfärbungen – ähnlich wie bei uns, wo man ja meist den Hessen oder Schwaben, den Rheinländer oder Bayern bereits am Tonfall erkennen kann. Sie werden auch gemerkt haben, daß beim Reden häufig verkürzte Sätze vorkommen, oder Sätze, die den Regeln der englischen Syntax nicht genau folgen, weil sich der Sprecher z.B. mehr auf den Inhalt dessen, was er mitteilen wollte, konzentriert hat als auf die Grammatik. Auch dies können wir in unserer eigenen Sprache häufig beobachten. Spontanes Reden und überlegtes Schreiben sind eben zwei Paar Stiefel. (Vgl. Telekolleg II, Deutsch, Bd. 1, S. 62 ff.)

Damit Sie nun lernen, mit *allen* Sprechern des Englischen zu kommunizieren, und das heißt vor allem auch: gesprochenes (Alltags-)Englisch zu verstehen, werden wir Ihnen mit Beginn dieses Trimesters „ungefiltertes" Englisch bieten. Statt der mit Schauspielern realisierten Spielszenen werden wir Ihnen jetzt in kurzen *Dokumentarfilmen* Menschen aus der britischen Alltagswirklichkeit vorführen, die so reden, wie ihnen der Schnabel gewachsen ist. Auch im Begleitbuch werden Sie Texte finden, die nicht von Sprachlehrern für Anfänger geschrieben wurden, sondern die britische Autoren für britische Leser verfaßt haben.

Vielleicht wird jetzt der eine oder andere von Ihnen sagen: Natürlich wollen wir nicht nur „Schulenglisch" lernen, aber auf „ungefiltertes" Englisch sind wir noch nicht genügend vorbereitet. Keine Sorge! Wir muten Ihnen keinen Sprung ins kalte Wasser zu. Die Studioteile zwischen den Dokumentarfilmen werden Sie Schritt für Schritt auf den „Ernstfall" vorbereiten, d.h. auf die Begegnung mit dem Englischen, wie es heute im Vereinigten Königreich (*United Kingdom*) tatsächlich gesprochen wird. Und auch dieses Begleitbuch wird Ihnen vielfache Hilfen bieten. Mehr dazu sagen wir Ihnen im übernächsten Abschnitt.

Landeskunde: „Crossing Borders"

Die Form des Dokumentarfilms haben wir nicht nur gewählt, um Ihnen Gelegenheit zu geben, sich in gesprochenes (Alltags-)Englisch hineinzuhören. Wir wollen Ihnen in den *units* 27 bis 39 zugleich eine Einführung in die britische Landeskunde vermitteln, d.h. wir wollen *dokumentieren*, wie die Menschen im heutigen *United Kingdom* leben, wie sie arbeiten, was sie in ihrer Freizeit tun, was ihnen Spaß macht und was ihnen Sorgen bereitet.

Die Lehrpläne für das Fach Englisch schreiben Landeskunde zwingend vor – aus guten Gründen, denn den Charakter einer Sprache und ihre Feinheiten kann man nur dann wirklich erfassen, wenn man auch etwas über die Menschen weiß, die diese Sprache sprechen. Denn wie Menschen leben, wie sie miteinander umgehen, wie sie denken und fühlen, das alles spiegelt sich in ihrer Sprache wider, wie umgekehrt die Sprache, mit der ein Mensch aufwächst, seine Art des Denkens und Fühlens beeinflußt. (Vgl. TK II, Deutsch, Bd. 1, S. 73 ff.)

Natürlich können wir Ihnen nicht in 13 Sendungen und auf etwas über hundert Buchseiten ein umfassendes Bild des Briten bieten – nicht nur, weil Ihre Zeit und der uns zur Verfügung stehende Raum dafür nicht ausreichen, sondern vor allem, weil es *den* Briten genausowenig gibt wie *den* Deutschen, *den* Amerikaner oder *den* Japaner. Es gibt im *United Kingdom*, wie in jedem anderen Land der Erde, Frauen und Männer, Junge und Alte, Arme und Reiche, Optimisten und Pessimisten, Engagierte und Gleichgültige. Nur ist das Mischungsverhältnis nicht in jedem Land das gleiche.

Im Falle des *United Kingdom* kommt hinzu, daß wir es nicht mit *einem* Land zu tun haben, sondern mit mehreren Ländern, die sich im Laufe der Geschichte mal mehr, mal weniger freiwillig zusammengeschlossen haben, deren Bewohner – Engländer, Schotten, Waliser, Nordiren – sich aber bis heute viel von ihrer nationalen Eigenart bewahrt haben. So werden wir bei unserer Erkundungsfahrt häufig Grenzen zu überqueren haben: vom europäischen Festland über den Kanal, von England nach Wales, nach Schottland, nach Nordirland; aber auch unsichtbare Grenzen, die quer durch die britische Gesellschaft verlaufen: Grenzen zwischen den Klassen, zwischen Alteingesessenen und Zuwanderern aus den Commonwealth-Ländern, zwischen Protestanten und Katholiken, und nicht zuletzt auch Sprachgrenzen. Wir hielten diesen Aspekt des *Crossing Borders* für so wichtig, daß wir den aus Yorkshire stammenden und in Wales lebenden Sänger und Dichter *Jake Thackray* gebeten haben, uns zu diesem Thema ein Lied zu schreiben. Dieses Lied, dessen Text Sie in *unit* 39 nachlesen können, wird uns durch alle 13 Sendungen begleiten.

Ihre Reisebegleiterin durch das *United Kingdom* wird *Linda Goodwin* sein, eine Amerikanerin, die im Nordosten der USA aufgewachsen ist, dort, wo das *American English (AE)* dem *British English (BE)* noch am ähnlichsten ist. Da Linda schon seit Jahren als Lehrerin in München arbeitet, ist sie mit der deutschen Denk- und Lebensweise recht gut vertraut. Deshalb entsprechen auch viele der Fragen, die sie ihren Gesprächspartnern im *United Kingdom* gestellt hat, genau den Fragen, die Sie selbst stellen würden.

Hinweise zur Mitarbeit

Wir haben versprochen, daß wir Sie bei Ihrer ersten Begegnung mit „ungefiltertem" Englisch nicht ohne Hilfe lassen. Die größte und wichtigste Hilfe muß aber von Ihnen selbst kommen: Versuchen Sie von Anfang an, mit der richtigen Einstellung an die Begegnung mit der englischen Alltagssprache heranzugehen: Konzentrieren Sie sich beim Mitverfolgen der Sendungen ganz auf *gist comprehension*, d.h. auf das Erfassen des Kerns der jeweiligen Aussagen. Niemand erwartet von Ihnen, daß Sie gesprochene Texte so bis in alle Einzelheiten hinein verstehen wie einen Text, der gedruckt vor Ihnen liegt und den Sie sich in Ihrem eigenen Lesetempo und mit Hilfe eines Wörterbuchs erarbeiten können. Werden Sie also nicht unruhig, wenn Sie den einen oder anderen Ausdruck oder – in den ersten *units* – sogar ganze Sätze nicht verstehen. Zum Erreichen des „Klassenziels" genügt es, wenn Sie die wichtigsten Aussagen einer Sendung richtig erfassen und sinngemäß wiedergeben können.

Sie werden sehen, daß es Ihnen relativ rasch gelingt, sich in die englische Alltagssprache hineinzuhören. Sie werden auch feststellen, daß Ihnen dabei die Fernsehbilder helfen: Die jeweilige Gesprächssituation (wer spricht wann und wo mit wem?), das Mienenspiel und die Gebärdensprache der Gesprächspartner geben Ihnen Hinweise auf das, worüber gesprochen wird. Verfolgen Sie die Sendungen also mit offenen *Ohren und Augen*!

Hilfen in den Sendungen

Damit es Ihnen etwas leichter fällt, die Dokumentationen über das *United Kingdom* zu verfolgen, haben wir sie in zwei Einheiten von je 7-8 Minuten aufgeteilt. Vor jedem dieser Dokumentarteile gibt Ihnen Ihr „*tele-teacher*" *Paul J. Dine* eine kurze Einführung und erklärt Wörter und Redewendungen, die für das Verständnis wichtig, Ihnen aber vielleicht noch unbekannt sind. Die letzten Minuten jeder Sendung sollen Ihnen bei der Prüfungsvorbereitung helfen: Da bieten wir Ihnen Übungen an, die an das in den Dokumentarteilen Gezeigte und Gesagte anknüpfen und die den Aufgaben ähnlich sind, die Ihnen bei der Hauptprüfung gestellt werden.

> Aufbauschema der Sendungen:
>
> 1. Einführung (Studio)
> 2. Dokumentation (1. Teil, Film)
> 3. Überleitung (Studio)
> 4. Dokumentation (2. Teil, Film)
> 5. Übungen (Studio)

Hilfen im Begleitbuch

Damit Sie die Sendungen bequem vor- und nacharbeiten können, bieten wir Ihnen in diesem Begleitbuch zu jedem Dokumentarteil (Abschnitte A und B):

– Eine Einführung in das jeweilige Thema. (Diesen Abschnitt sollten Sie nach Möglichkeit *vor* der Sendung lesen. Er erleichtert Ihnen das Verständnis!).

– Eine Zusammenfassung des Inhalts der Dokumentation (*contents of the documentary film*). Als kleine Verständnishilfe haben wir in diese *contents* nicht nur den wesentlichen Wortschatz, sondern auch schwierigere Dialogpassagen aus den betreffenden Fernsehsendungen aufgenommen.

– Ergänzungstexte, d.h. ein oder zwei Auszüge aus englischen Zeitungen oder Büchern, die das in der Dokumentation Gesagte und Gezeigte um weitere Aspekte ergänzen. (Diese mit einem Sternchen gekennzeichneten Texte gehören nicht zum „Pflichtteil" Ihrer Aufgaben, können also bei Zeitnot übersprungen und später in Ruhe nachgelesen werden.)

Im Anschluß an die einzelnen Texte haben wir Ihnen in der Regel einige Fragen gestellt. Diese *questions* sollen Ihre Aufmerksamkeit auf wichtige Aussagen in der Sendung lenken bzw. Ihnen überprüfen helfen, ob Sie die wesentlichen Aussagen der Texte in ihrem Kern verstanden haben.

Um Ihnen allzu häufiges Nachschlagen in Ihrem Wörterbuch zu ersparen, haben wir den Texten bereits Worterklärungen in englischer Sprache angefügt und in schwierigeren Fällen die Lautschrift angegeben. Außerdem finden Sie im Schlußteil dieses Buches noch eine alphabetisch geordnete zweisprachige *wordlist*.

Unter der Überschrift „*Focus on language*" (Abschnitt C) beschäftigen wir uns am Ende jeder *unit* – analog zur Sendung – noch einmal mit einem bestimmten grammatikalischen Thema: Die kurzen Erläuterungen sind als „Erinnerungshilfe" für Sie gedacht, die daran anschließenden Übungen (*exercises*) sollten Sie gezielt zur Prüfungsvorbereitung benützen.

Die Lösungsvorschläge zu *questions* und *exercises* haben wir bewußt im Anschluß an die letzte *unit* gesetzt. Wir möchten Sie in Ihrem eigenen Interesse dazu einladen, die Aufgaben zunächst selbständig zu lösen, statt Sie dazu zu verleiten, gleich auf unsere Vorschläge zu schauen.

Wir hoffen, daß Ihnen die Mitarbeit im Telekolleg II/Englisch mit den hier gebotenen Hilfen nicht schwer wird, daß es Ihnen vielmehr Freude macht, von Sendung zu Sendung mehr Sicherheit im Umgang mit der englischen Sprache zu gewinnen und jedesmal Neues und Interessantes über das *United Kingdom* zu erfahren.

Wir würden uns besonders freuen, wenn Ihnen dieser Kurs Lust darauf macht, selbst den Kanal zu überqueren, Ihre eigenen Erfahrungen zu sammeln und Ihre Englischkenntnisse praktisch zu erproben.

Dieter Buttjes
Paul J. Dine
Lothar Humburg

Erläuterung der im Buch verwendeten Abkürzungen:
adj. = adjective
n = noun
v = verb

Linda Goodwin und Paul Dine im Studio vor den Flaggen von Schottland, England, Nordirland und Wales; in der Mitte der *Union Jack*.

Some notes on British flags and on the introductory music of this course

The flag of the United Kingdom of Great Britain and Northern Ireland is officially called the **Union Flag** because it combines the flags of three countries united under one rule:

– the red cross of St George on a white ground (England)
– the white diagonal cross of St Andrew on a blue ground (Scotland)
– the red diagonal cross of St Patrick (Ireland).

The first Union Flag, in 1606, combined the crosses of St George and St Andrew. At that time, King James I had united **England** and **Scotland** under his rule. The cross of St Patrick was not added until 1801, following the union of Great Britain with **Ireland**. The cross remains in the Union Flag, although now only Northern Ireland forms part of the United Kingdom, while southern Ireland is an independent republic.

The flag of **Northern Ireland** is the cross of St George, with a six-pointed star at its centre, representing the six counties of the country. The red star stands for Ulster. On top of the star is the Royal crown.

The flag of **Wales** is a red dragon on a green and white ground. It does not appear in the Union Flag because, when the first Union Flag was made up in 1606, Wales was already united with England and no longer a separate monarchy.

So, you see, the British flags which we display in the studio do not merely serve as a nice background. They also tell you quite a few things about the four countries which form the United Kingdom.

By the way: The Union Flag is more commonly known as the **Union Jack**. This "nickname" was probably introduced by the Royal Navy. Their ships carry the small Union Flag at the jack-staff, which is at the bows.

Now for the music which you will hear at the beginning and end of each TV unit of this course: It is taken from the first of six military marches for orchestra, called the *Pomp and Circumstance Marches*, by the British composer Sir Edward Elgar (1857-1934). We chose it because it is well known in the United Kingdom, and many British people would like to have it for a national anthem, instead of *God save the Queen*. The words which go with the music were written by A.C. Benson (1862-1925) as a coronation ode for King Edward VII. The chorus runs like this:

> Land of Hope and Glory,
> Mother of the free,
> How shall we extol thee
> Who are born of thee?
>
> Wider still and wider
> Shall thy bounds be set.
> God who made thee mighty
> Make thee mightier yet!

Words
represent – stand for; *display* (v) – show; *bows* – forward part of a ship; *national anthem* /ˈænθəm/ – the official song of a nation; *extol* – praise highly; *thee, thy* – old singular forms of "you" and "your"; *bounds* – borders.

Dover and the Garden of England — Unit 27

A

Dover's great past and its uncertain future 🎧

The White Horse and the "Tidy Ruin"

Before we start our tour, we should remember that we are not just going to visit **Great Britain** (which is the name for England, Wales and Scotland together) but the whole of the **United Kingdom**, which includes Northern Ireland. Its full name is in fact the **United Kingdom of Great Britain and Northern Ireland.**

The shortest sea crossing from the Continent is between Calais and **Dover**. Here the Channel is only 21 miles wide (or just under 34 kilometres) and in fact, on a clear day, you can see France from the top of the famous **White Cliffs of Dover**.

Dover has been one of the main gateways to Britain from Roman times to the present day. It has always been so important to the rulers of Britain that they fortified the hill above the town to protect the country against invasion from the sea at this point. A number of buildings have survived from the various centuries to remind us of this.

So, for example, you can see there the **Pharos** /'feərɒs/, which was built by the Romans. "Pharos" is a Greek word for lighthouse, and the Romans used to light a beacon or signal fire on top of it to guide their ships across the Channel from the Continent. They also used it as a watchtower so that the soldiers on duty there would be able to spot enemy ships while they were still a long way off.

Another reminder of how important Dover has always been is the little church of **St Mary in Castro** – "in castro" is Latin for "in the castle" – which stands next to the Pharos and was built here by the Saxons around the year 1000 at the centre of their fortress on the hill above Dover.

When William the Conqueror became King of England in 1066, one of the first things he did was to have the fortifications at Dover strengthened. And during the next century, one of his successors started to build the castle that we see there today when we arrive by ferry. The **keep**, or big central tower, of **Dover Castle** goes back to that time.

Dover is also one of the main ports for people wanting to go to the Continent with their cars and for lorries transporting goods to and from the U.K. This means that some 30,000 or more of the inhabitants of Dover and the surrounding countryside are dependent in some way on the port. This also explains why the people of Dover are very worried about the plans to build a **Channel Tunnel** or **Chunnel**, as it is often called.

If the Chunnel is built, a lot of people will be out of work at Dover. The tunnel will end some 7 miles to the south-west of Dover further inland, so that it will bypass Dover (and nearby Folkestone as well).

However, it is not just the people of Dover who are against building the Chunnel. Since the Chunnel will be a rail connection to the Continent and shorten the crossing to and from France only by some 30 minutes at the most, many other people also ask whether it is really worth investing billions of pounds to save so little time. They are also afraid of the damage the Channel Tunnel could cause to the environment. All it would mean, they maintain, is that still bigger car parks and even more roads and railway lines would spoil this very beautiful part of the country still further.

Of course, there are a large number of people who are in favour of building the tunnel. They say it would lower the cost of crossing the Channel not just for the ordinary car driver but for British industry as well. They point out that the sea crossing is not only expensive, it is also very inconvenient. On the new rail link drivers and their passengers would be able to stay in their cars. And it goes without saying that no one would have to be afraid of being seasick any more! Another argument is that the Chunnel would finally make the British realize that they really do belong to Europe and that in future the countries of the European Community will have to sink or swim together. That is why it is so important that the United Kingdom's industrial centres should be directly linked to the key EEC markets on the Continent.

Words

fortify – you fortify a building when you make it strong against attack. That means you have provided the building with *fortifications*, that is with strong walls and towers. The fortified building is then known as a *fort* or, especially if it is big, a *fortress*; *survive* – continue to exist; *lighthouse* – nowadays a tall tower with a flashing light at the top to guide ships or warn them about dangerous rocks, etc.; *beacon* – a light or fire used as a signal; *successor* – a person who takes over a position or office formerly held by someone else; *keep* (n) – the main central part of a castle; *bypass* (v) – go round or not go through a town; *environment* – the natural conditions, such as air, water and countryside, in which we live. A person who tries to stop the environment from being spoilt is called an *environmentalist*; *link* (n) – something which connects things. The Chunnel will provide a *rail link* and not a *road link* between the U.K. and the Continent; *European Community* – the European Economic Community (abbreviated to EEC), which is sometimes called the *Common Market*.

Questions

1. Why has Dover always been such an important town and port in British history?
2. Dover Castle has sometimes been seen as a symbol of Britain's island independence. In your opinion is this an important consideration nowadays in view of the U.K.'s membership of the EEC?
3. Do you think it is a good idea to build a tunnel between the U.K. and the Continent?

Contents of the documentary film, part A

After reaching Calais, Linda got on the car ferry to Dover. Soon after she went up to the bridge, where Captain Mike Western had agreed to talk to her. After welcoming her aboard, Mike Western then invited her into the wheelhouse. There Linda began asking him questions.
First she asked him how many people crossed the Channel by car ferry every year. And Mike Western told her that about 14 million passengers and some 3 million cars a year crossed the Channel from Dover.

Linda then wanted to know whether the Channel Tunnel or Chunnel could change all that. Mike replied that he hoped the Chunnel would not be built at all, because so far the shipping operators had managed very well to keep pace with the increase in traffic levels over the years.
Nevertheless, Mike Western admitted that the possibility that they could lose their jobs was at the back of all their minds on the ship. Why? Because they had all been trained to operate a ship and that was a different kind of work to the type of job that would be involved in the Channel Tunnel. As the car ferry drew closer to Dover, Linda had her first view of the famous White Cliffs of Dover and then of Dover and its port.

Linda's first stop in Dover was a very old pub called The White Horse. Inside the pub she talked to Charles Willet, the publican. Like Charles, Linda is also a Dovorian, because she is from Dover in the State of Vermont in the United States of America.
After closing time, Charles Willet took Linda up to Dover Castle, starting out from the Tidy Ruin next to The White Horse. On the way they talked about the changes that had taken place in Dover, especially since the War. Linda also asked him what he felt about the Castle:

> Linda: So, Charles, what does the Castle mean for you as a Dovorian?
> Charles: Well, as a Dovorian, I'm very proud of it. It's part of my town. It's been part of my life for nearly 60 years. But I am also very proud of it because it signifies the solidness, the solidity of this country and the island we live in.
> Linda: Well, it's kept people out for a long time, hasn't it?
> Charles: It certainly has. And the very fact that it's preserved in this fashion and looked after in this fashion is a thing of great pride to me as well.

Charles then showed Linda the church of St Mary in Castro, which he said was early Saxon, possibly on a Roman foundation. It had been used as a garrison church for hundreds of years, apart from the time when it had been used as a coal store or cellar.

The structure next to the church, he explained, was known as the Pharos. This had been built by the Romans as a lighthouse: they lit a beacon on the top to guide their galleys safely across the Channel to Dover.

They finally went to the top of the keep, where Linda got her first view of the country she had come to explore.

Words

car ferry – a ferry is a boat that takes people and things across a river or other narrow waterway. A car ferry is one that can transport cars and other motor vehicles as well; *bridge* – the raised area at the front of a ship where the captain and other officers stand when on duty; *welcome aboard* – receive someone with pleasure on a ship or aircraft; *wheelhouse* – the room on a ship where the wheel to steer the ship is; *shipping operators* – the people or companies which control, manage and run the ferries; *manage* – succeed in doing something; *keep pace with* – keep up with something or someone, not get left behind; *traffic level* – the amount of traffic, the number of vehicles; Captain Western maintains that the shipping companies have always succeeded in keeping up the demand for their services; *involved in* – connected with; *publican* – the person who runs or manages a public house; *Dovorian* – an inhabitant of Dover; *closing time* – the time when by law a publican is no longer allowed to serve drinks and has to close the pub; *The Tidy Ruin* – a very old church destroyed during World War II and never rebuilt; *solidity* – the quality of being solid, i.e. dependable and durable; *preserve* (v) – keep in good condition; *look after* – take care of someone or something; *garrison* – the group of soldiers living in and defending a town or castle; *coal store* – a place or room to keep coal in. As this was often below ground, it was also known as a *coal cellar*; *structure* – building; *galley* – a ship which was rowed by slaves or prisoners.

Questions

4. A car ferry also has some big advantages. Can you think of the main ones?
5. If you have been to a pub in the U.K., you will have noticed some important differences to places where you get a drink in your own country. What are they?

*A 200-year-old dream

Napoleon had a dream. He proposed in 1802 that a tunnel be dug under the neck of water that connects the Atlantic Ocean and the North Sea – and that separates Britain and France in so many ways. Britons call it the English Channel. French call it **La Manche** (the Sleeve). To Napoleon, it was "a ditch that will be leaped whenever one has the boldness to try".

He dreamed, but he did not try. War with England resumed in 1803, and his idea was dropped. Since then dozens of other tunnel projects have been drawn up, debated and, in a few cases, partly dug. Britain's House of Commons has debated the matter a total of 38 times in the past two centuries. Most of the schemes have vanished like the legendary Channel fog. Today, as it has for milleniums, the Channel remains a formidable barrier, physical and psychological, between Britain and the rest of the Continent. ... By the early 1990s, England may be an island no longer.

(*Time*, January 20, 1986.)

B
The county of Kent 👓

Thatched cottage in the Garden of England

The United Kingdom is divided up into counties, and each county has its own characteristic landscape and countryside.

The county of Kent, for instance, is known as the **Garden of England**. Because the soil was good, the climate mild, and the rainfall regular but moderate, the Romans planted orchards and vineyards there, and, right up to the present day, Kent has always been famous for its fruit, particularly for the apples and pears, the plums, cherries and strawberries grown there. To give just one example, there are over 32,000 acres of apple orchards in Kent. Hops, used in the making of beer, and vegetables are also cultivated there.

Typical of the countryside in Kent are the green meadows, the many trees and hedges, the herds of sheep and cattle, and finally lovely old houses often with thatched roofs. The road network is good, so that a large number of people living in Kent commute to and from London every day.

One of the surprises about Kent is that it covers one of England's smaller but important coalfields. The National Coal Board (NCB) operates three coalmines here at Snowdown, Tilmanstone and Betteshanger, all just a few miles from Dover. Betteshanger Colliery, for example, produces about 400,000 tonnes of coal a year. Just as in other countries around the world, the British coal industry is going through very difficult times.

Words

county – a subdivision of territory in the U.K. which is important for local government purposes; *landscape* /'lænskeɪp/ – a wide view of scenery in the country; *countryside* /'kʌntrɪsaɪd/ – land outside the towns and cities, a country area; *soil* – the top layer or covering of earth in which plants grow; the ground; *mild* – not extreme or hard; gentle; *moderate* – neither too much nor too little; *orchard* /'ɔ:tʃəd/ – a field or part of a garden where fruit trees grow; *vineyard* /'vɪnjəd/ – a piece of land planted with vines (= plants that produce grapes); *meadow* /'medəʊ/ – grassland on which cattle, sheep, horses, etc., feed; *thatched roof* – a roof made of straw or other dried plants; *commute* /kə'mju:t/ – travel a long distance regularly between one's home and one's place of work; *coalfield* – an area where a lot of coal is; *National Coal Board* – the nationalized or state-owned institution which manages the British coalmines; *colliery* – the coalmine with all its buildings and machinery; *tonne* /tʌn/ – a metric ton consisting of 1000 kilos (a British ton is 2240 pounds and a US ton is 2000 pounds!).

Contents of the documentary film, part B

After Dover and Dover Castle, Linda continued her journey through the county of Kent, the Garden of England. A lot of what she saw here reminded her very much of New England in her own country, but what she had come here to see was not the countryside, but Betteshanger Colliery. Here Charles Willet had put her in touch with Peter Heap, Press Officer of the National Coal Board. While he was showing her around the colliery, Peter Heap told Linda that coalmines around the world had been going through a bad patch, largely because of the politics and economics of the oil industry. He continued:

> "In the past 3 or 4 years the pressures on coal prices around the world have been such that the traded market prices have been falling very rapidly. The National Coal Board's policy has been to reduce costs as rapidly as possible in order to compete with imported coal and fuel oil.
> And there has been a rapid process of pit closures after the end of the miners' strike in 1985, which is helping to reduce costs and to eliminate old high-cost mining capacity.
> Coal reserves are enormous. In Great Britain alone we have enough coal to work at our present rate of extraction for more than 300 years. And there are vast untapped reserves in China, India and the Soviet Union."

After her talk with Peter Heap, Linda was introduced to Norman Dans, the chief engineer at the colliery. They first went into the lamp cabin, where she saw the miners putting the cap-lamps on their helmets before going down into the mine. Norman Dans told Linda that he was in fact from Wales, had started mining in the Midlands and come down to work in Kent because of the lack of opportunities and jobs in Wales. Linda also learnt from Norman that Betteshanger Colliery had two shafts, 600 metres deep. It took the miners only 30 seconds to ride the shaft but approximately three quarters of an hour to reach their place of work down in the mine.

Words
press officer – person whose job it is to keep up good relations with the newspapers and magazines; *go through a bad patch* – experience a time of trouble or misfortune, experience difficult times; *pressure* /'preʃə/ – outside influence; *traded market price* – the actual price a series of buyers paid for coal; *reduce costs* – lower the price of producing coal; *compete* /kəm'pi:t/ *with* – have a chance against or even beat the price asked by other sellers; *fuel* /'fjʊəl/ – something used to produce heat or power by burning; *closure* – the act of closing a coalmine forever (Pit is another word for coalmine);

high-cost mining capacity – coalmines that produce coal too expensively; *rate of extraction* – the speed of getting coal out of the earth; *reserves* – the coal still in the earth; *untapped reserves* – the amount of coal still in the earth and so far not extracted; *cap-lamp* – lamp a miner wears on his protective hat or helmet; *ride the shaft* – descend (by lift) down the long passage leading to the underground levels where the coal is mined.

Questions
6. The coal mining industry is going through difficult times all over the world. Give some of the main reasons.
7. Why do you think that there are fewer opportunities and jobs in Wales for a mining engineer like Norman Dans?

*The miners' strike

On March 5, 1985, with bands playing and heads held high, the striking miners marched back to their pits. For the defeated strikers it was a day of bitterness and humiliation. For the government of Prime Minister Margaret Thatcher it was the moment of victory. The strike ended a year almost to the day after it had begun with the announcement by the National Coal Board (NCB) of a plan to close 20 uneconomic pits and thereby make redundant some 20,000 of the industry's 186,000 workers. Throughout the bitter and often violent dispute, Arthur Scargill, president of the National Union of Mineworkers (NUM), had insisted that there was no such thing as an uneconomic pit. But the strike was about more than the economic future of the British coal industry. It was about the constitutional and political authority of the government; it was about the rule of law over disorder; and it was about the cohesion of the Labour movement – the Trades Union Congress (TUC) and the Labour Party – and the power of the trade unions.

For Scargill the strike was a single battle in a revolutionary class struggle. This viewpoint had given the strike a political character from the outset and had increased the government's determination to win and to be seen to win decisively. Not least this was because folk memories of the events of 1974 – when the Conservative Party government of Edward Heath had been destroyed at the hands of the miners, or had perhaps destroyed itself with their aid – were still strong. For Thatcher the strike was also a trial of will.

By the beginning of the year the outcome of the dispute was no longer in doubt. The miners were effectively beaten. Coal stocks were more than sufficient to see the winter through; not an electric light bulb had been extinguished in contrast to the blackouts of 1974, when industry had been reduced to a three-day working week. Moreover, once the New Year arrived the drift back to work of defeated or disaffected miners gathered pace until, toward the end of February, the NCB could claim that more than 50% of the miners were at work, including the 26% . . . who had refused to join the strike in the first place. Scargill remained recalcitrant to the very last. In the end, at a delegate conference of the NUM, the miners voted by the narrowest margin for a return to work without any terms at all. In effect, it was unconditional surrender. Nevertheless, Scargill claimed victory. "All our future struggles will be stronger as a result," he declared. Few other leaders of the Labour movement agreed with him.

(*Encyclopaedia Britannica*, 1986 Book of the Year, p. 537.)

Words
Trades Union Congress (generally known as the TUC) – the association of British trade unions; *coal stocks* – supplies of coal; *disaffected* – politically discontented; here: discontented with the policy of the NUM.

C
Focus on language: Spoken English

In units 27-39 you are going to hear a lot of **spoken** English. The grammar the speakers use in our films will not cause you any difficulty, because it is the same grammar that you have learnt. In fact, the grammar you have been taught is nothing else but a description or summary of the English actually used by native speakers of the language.

However, since we are taking you to all parts of the United Kingdom, what will cause you some difficulty will be the different accents you hear. Like Linda, you will find some accents easier to understand than others. Since almost all native speakers of English speak it with some degree of an accent, the sooner you get used to listening to English spoken with an accent the better.

Another difficulty about spoken English is that native speakers shorten forms (e.g. "I'd like to…" for "I would like to…") and swallow syllables (e.g. in "go and see" the "and" is swallowed and becomes something that sounds like "'n"). Above all, in conversation native speakers of English do not repeat things unnecessarily. So, for example, when Linda asked Captain Western in the first documentary film, "Captain Western, could you tell me about how many people cross this Channel by car ferry every year", he did not answer, "From Dover about 14 million passengers and about 3 million cars cross the Channel by car ferry every year", but simply said, "From Dover about 14 million passengers and about 3 million cars." There was absolutely no need for him to repeat the words of the second half of Linda's question; his answer was perfectly clear without that.

At times, you might find some of the English you hear in our documentary films difficult to understand. But don't give up. Remember that practice makes perfect. You can be absolutely certain that any effort and hard work you invest now will be rewarded. The reward will be that in the end you will be able to understand real live native speakers speaking the real English of everyday life! And that surely was the goal you set yourself when you started learning the language.

Exercises
1. Here are parts of actual conversations Linda had in the first documentary film in unit 27. However, we have added the parts of the sentences which the speakers in the actual conversations did not repeat from earlier statements or questions.
   Please cross out the parts which you think are unnecessary repetitions.

   a) Linda: I'd like to go to the Castle.
      Charles: As soon as we close, my dear, I'll take you to the Castle.
      Linda: I'd love to go there. Would you really take me up to the Castle?
      Charles: Yes, certainly I'll take you up to the Castle.
   b) Linda: Do you know I'm a Dovorian myself? Dover, Vermont. Have you ever heard of the place?

	Charles:	I have heard of the place. I think you've got two or three Dovers in America, haven't you? But they're not as good as this one, of course.
c)	Linda:	So you're not from Dover?
	Man in pub:	No... Well, I'm from Kent but not from Dover. I've lived in Dover a long time.
	Charles:	You've lived here too long, if you ask me.
d)	Linda:	Well, it's kept people out for a long time, hasn't it?
	Charles:	It certainly has kept people out for a long time.

2. Please say which words or phrases correspond to the following definitions.

   a) to make a building strong against attack;
   b) a person who takes over a position or office formerly held by someone else;
   c) a boat that takes not just people and things across water but cars and other motor vehicles as well;
   d) to care for someone or something;
   e) to try to find someone or something;
   f) a field or part of a garden where fruit trees grow;
   g) to travel a long distance regularly between one's home and one's place of work;
   h) to experience a time of trouble or misfortune, to experience difficult times.

3. Please translate into German as literally as possible and as freely as necessary.

   The county of Kent, for instance, is known as the Garden of England. Because the soil was good, the climate mild, and the rainfall regular but moderate, the Romans planted orchards and vineyards there, and, right up to the present day, Kent has always been famous for its fruit, particularly for the apples and pears, the plums, cherries and strawberries grown there...
   Typical of the countryside in Kent are the green meadows, the many trees and hedges, the herds of sheep and cattle, and finally lovely old houses often with thatched roofs. The road network is good, so that a large number of people living in Kent commute to and from London every day.

Markets in London   Unit 28

A
The Thames and the City of London

The Thames Flood Barrier

The Thames, England's principal river, is 210 miles (338 km) long, and, on its way to the North Sea, flows through a number of places well-known throughout the world, like the university town of Oxford (where the river is called the Isis!) and Windsor with its major tourist attraction, the royal castle. However, it is not until it reaches London, the capital, that the river takes on real significance, since London could never have developed into the important town it has in fact become without the Thames. We should never forget that the main reason a town grew up here in the first place was because it was possible to build both a bridge and a port at this point on the River Thames. The bridge shortened distances for land travel and meant that in time London inevitably became the centre of an extensive road network; the port improved connections with the countries across the Channel and made it possible for ships to enter and leave with the tides.
However, while the tides were a great advantage to the port of London, they have over the centuries also brought dangerous floods at times to the town. Every now and then an unusually high tide, called a surge tide, comes down the North Sea and enters the Thames. One does not need a great deal of imagination to realize what a disaster it would be if modern London were flooded. It was to make such a catastrophe forever impossible that the **Thames Flood Barrier** was constructed.

Since the destinies of London and the River Thames have always been so closely linked, it is not surprising that almost everything of interest and importance in London is located on or near the river, so that a boat trip to London up the Thames provides an extremely good introduction to the capital.

Even if the drawbridge at the centre of **Tower Bridge** is now rarely raised to allow large ships to pass through because London has lost its importance as a port, Tower Bridge not only remains a world-famous landmark of London; it is also the gateway to the heart of London, the famous Square Mile, which starts here on the north bank of the Thames.

The Square Mile is where London began, and it is here that most of the history of the town has taken place. For instance, the Square Mile is almost coterminous with the town the Romans built here during the first century as the centre of their British province. It was here, too, that William the Conqueror set up his capital when he became king of England in 1066. To protect his new capital from invaders but also to deter the Londoners from rebelling against their new king, he built the Tower of London, which, in the more than 900 years since then, has been used as a fortress, a palace, a zoo, a mint and a prison.

As a final example of a historical event connected with the Square Mile, it was within its boundaries that the Great Fire of London broke out in the year 1666. This is said to have been the worst fire to devastate a major European city in peace time since the terrible conflagration which occurred in Rome under the Emperor Nero.

The Square Mile is still extremely important today, because it is also the site of the **City of London**, one of the leading international financial centres in the world. Here, within a very small area, which you can walk across in some twenty minutes, a large proportion of the money business of the world is still transacted.

There are a great many financial institutions concentrated in the City, so we will mention just a few of them here. The Bank of England, the central bank of the United Kingdom, is located there, and so are the head offices of the Big Four among the British banks. More than 450 foreign banks are represented in the City, too, although rents there are the highest in the world after Hong Kong! Right next door to the Bank of England you will find the Stock Exchange, where stocks and shares are bought and sold.

Lloyd's of London is also situated in the City. Lloyd's is still the largest insurance market in the world where things like ships, aeroplanes and even spacecraft are insured. But it is also famous for insuring very unusual risks, like insuring a pop group against anything that could happen to it on a concert tour – for example, one of the group might fall ill, their musical instruments could be stolen or their fans damage one of the concert halls.

In recent years big changes have taken place and are still taking place in the City. It is hoped that all these changes will help the City keep pace with the changing needs of the international business community.

Words

principal – main, chief, most important; *significance* – importance, value, meaning; *tide* – the rise and fall of the water of the sea. We talk about a high tide and a low tide. A surge tide is a high tide which is particularly strong and fast-moving; *flood* – water overflowing into or covering a place which is usually dry; *barrier* – something erected to prevent people or things (here: water) from entering or moving forward; *destiny* – fate or fortune; *drawbridge* – a bridge that can be pulled up; *landmark* – object or structure regarded as characteristic of a place or locality; *coterminous* – having the same border, being within the same limits; *deter* – discourage or restrain someone from doing something; *devastate* – destroy completely; *conflagration* – a very large and destructive fire; *transact* – do or conduct business; *stocks and shares* – shares in the capital of a company; *insure* – protect against loss of life, money, goods, etc.; *risk* (n) – danger.

Questions
1. What sort of serious things could happen, do you think, if London were flooded?
2. Why do you think London has lost its former importance as a port?

Contents of the documentary film, part A

After visiting Kent, Linda had decided to take a boat up the River Thames to London. The captain of the boat was a Londoner named John, who also acted as her guide.

They started their trip up the Thames at the Thames Barrier and then moved up river to Tower Bridge.

Linda:	Oh. Here's Tower Bridge.
John:	Yes, this is the famous gateway to London.
Linda:	Well, aren't we in London already?
John:	Well, you will be. When you go under here, you will be in the famous City of London, the Square Mile. And you'll notice the tremendous amount of change that is going on here, how they are altering buildings, new buildings going up.

And indeed, new buildings were going up everywhere and a lot of old wharfs and warehouses were being converted. One of them had been changed into a hospital but in the City most of them were being altered into office buildings. Further down river, he told her, they had given way mainly to flats and private houses.

Linda then saw New London Bridge and learnt that Old London Bridge had been taken apart stone by stone and then rebuilt in Lake Havasu in the State of Arizona in the USA. He also informed her that there were 26 bridges over the Thames up to Teddington, one of the outskirts of London, although there were lots more the further you went up the river.

When Linda asked how long he had been working on the Thames, John replied since 1949, a long time ago. Since then he had seen a lot of changes on the river. The River Thames had once been a thriving commercial river. On how clean the water of the Thames had become, John proudly told Linda:

> "Yes, it's said to be the clearest... cleanest commercial river in Europe. We've got about 130 varieties of fish at the moment, fish, eels.
> The wild life on it is prolific. We've got hawks. We've got ducks. We've got cranes. We've got everything on here at the moment, you know. It's really good, really good."

After leaving the boat, Linda then went up the Monument to look down at the City of London from above and to take some photographs. Afterwards she walked around the City and was just taking a photograph of the new Lloyd's building, when she met Albert Jones, who works in the City of London and offered to show her around.

Linda mentioned to Albert that she had expected to see more people in pin-striped suits and bowler hats and Albert told her that she would not see many bowler hats, especially when the weather was hot. Albert also agreed that the rents in the City of London were the highest after Hong Kong because, like Hong Kong, they had to fit a great deal into a small space. So many foreign banks had come to the City to do business, he went on, precisely because it was such a small area. There they had access to all sorts of markets – the insurance market, the money market, the stock market. And the fact that English was the world language of business was a great advantage, too.

Finally, Albert took her up 35 floors to the top of Britannic House, the headquarters of BP. On looking down, Linda remarked:

> Linda: Well, that square mile called the City down there must be getting too small for all the business that's done.
>
> Albert: Well, it looks small. But we fit an awful lot into a small space. But it does mean as well as building upwards, as you can see we're doing, we're having to make a lot of changes. Not just in the Stock Market this year, but in Lloyd's we have to accustom ourselves to new regulations. And one of the big changes that's going to happen is that the markets are going to come together, all under one roof.

Words

go on – take place or happen; *go up* – be built or constructed; *wharf* /wɔːf/ – (plural: wharfs or wharves) place where ships can be tied up to unload their goods; *warehouse* /ˈweəhaʊs/ – a building where things are stored before being sold or taken somewhere else (N.B. „Warenhaus" = department store); *take apart* – separate into pieces; *USA* – it is a peculiarity of John's English that he says "the US of A"; *thrive* /θraɪv/ – be successful, prosperous or healthy; *eel* – fish shaped like a snake and difficult to hold; *wild life* – birds and animals that live and grow in natural conditions; *prolific* – producing a lot of young; *hawk* – a bird which catches other birds and animals with its feet (claws); *crane* – a tall bird with long neck and long legs which walks in water and catches fish with its long beak; *bowler hat* – a round, hard hat (usually black); *fit* (v) – accommodate; make room or place for; *access* – entry, entrance, way in.

Question

3. As John and Linda go up the Thames by boat, what do you see that makes it clear that the River Thames is no longer a thriving commercial river?

*The Global Market

"In most areas of international business, London is competing for activities which could, in theory at least, be located almost anywhere in the world. On the world's financial markets, there is always room for a new competitor...

The City's geographical location has become an important advantage; it is close enough to Hong Kong and Singapore to open trading just before those Asian markets close – and yet an hour closer to New York than any rival European centre. The English language is an unquestionable advantage, as is the tradition of dealing, based on London's long history as a commercial trading centre. Then there is the fact that it is an easier place to live (particularly for Americans and Japanese) than Continental centres such as Brussels or Frankfurt. Europe probably has room for only one major international financial centre, and London has been lucky enough to get there first. London still has the most important single concentration of international financial markets in the world. To keep its edge will take more than luck and the English language. World financial markets are changing with extraordinary speed. London's main rivals, New York and Tokyo, are also each passing through a transformation... London has to find a way of turning its disadvantage – the dwindling relative size of the British economy – into an advantage by being more internationally-minded than its rivals. If at the same time it can continue to improve the service it offers to its British customers, then in the long run the whole economy will gain."

(From: H. McRae and F. Cairncross, *Capital City. London as a Financial Centre.* Methuen. London 1985, pp. 251-252.)

Words
trading – business of buying, selling and exchanging things. Another word for trading is *dealing*;
keep one's edge – stay ahead of others, remain better than others, maintain one's advantage.

Questions
4. In the three sections you have had so far in this chapter you have learnt a lot about the City of London. What advantages does the City of London have over other financial centres in Europe like Frankfurt and Brussels?
5. Suggest some of the things the City will have to do to keep its edge over its rivals?

B
London – a town of many markets ⊙⊙

Portobello Road

As we have seen, London had relatively small beginnings, the Roman town covering roughly the same area as the present-day Square Mile. However, even under the Romans, it was already a trading centre and market town. And around this original core, a number of towns, villages and hamlets grew up over the centuries and they had their own local marketplaces as well.

Since then, especially in modern times, London has grown bigger and bigger, and has slowly but surely swallowed up all those surrounding towns, villages and hamlets and become the enormous town it is today. The towns, villages and hamlets may have ceased to exist, but very often they have managed to maintain their individual characters and local traditions, and many of their marketplaces have survived, too. And it is this which makes London a town with numerous street markets, the two best known of which are probably Petticoat Lane in the East End and Portobello Road in West London.

Petticoat Lane is surely the most famous of London's street markets. It's mainly new and second-hand clothes that are sold there, but you can buy almost anything else there as well. Be careful if you go there, because Petticoat Lane has always been known for its pickpockets. Londoners will tell you jokingly that, if your watch is stolen at one end of the market, you should keep your eyes open at the other end, because it will almost certainly already be on sale there.

Portobello Road claims to be the world's best known market for antiques. During the week it is very quiet there and there is only a very small fruit and vegetable market along one part of it. On Saturdays, however, the whole street suddenly comes to life and is packed with people.

It may be true that the tourists have partially turned these two markets into big business. However, it is still a worthwhile experience to visit a London market, and there can be few better ways of discovering what a colourful and varied town London is.

Words

core – the most important or central part of anything; *hamlet* – a small village; *swallow up* – take in and cause to disappear; *pickpocket* – a person who steals things from people's pockets, especially in a crowd; *packed with people* – full of people, very crowded; *worthwhile* – worth doing, worth taking the trouble, rewarding.

Contents of the documentary film, part B

After visiting the famous City of London, Linda wanted to see one of London's numerous street markets. She chose to go to Portobello Road, where she wanted to visit a friend, Henry Gregory. Henry was very glad to see Linda because he needed her help for a couple of hours. He took her up the road to a second shop, where he first introduced her to his brother, Andy, and to John, the senior partner. In this second shop they specialized in jewellery and every Saturday they sold loads of stuff there. It was packed then, he told her, from morning till night. All the jewellery cost just £ 1. In fact, they did not sell just jewellery in the shop but other small antiques like toast racks, sugar pots, scales and other silver-plated articles. Linda protested that she had never worked as a saleslady before:

        Linda: But, Henry, I've never done this before.
        Henry: I don't care. You'll learn in about 2 minutes.
        Linda: And I don't know a thing about antiques.

| Henry: | You'll soon learn.
There's some change down there.
We're going to do down to the pub for a beer. You're in charge.
Good luck, Linda. |
|---|---|

Linda did good business but some of the people kept trying to get her to go down in price so that Linda had to tell them that the boss would be back in a little while and then they could have a word with him.

Later Linda returned to the main shop to talk with Henry. She told him that it had been great fun selling for him and that business had been excellent. She also had another question for Henry:

Linda:	Is it still possible for a person like me who doesn't know much about antiques to get bargains here?
Henry:	Yes. But you have to be a different kind of tourist. I see so many tourists coming down Portobello Road with their cameras, and their grannies, and their babies and . . . ! To buy a good thing you must look everywhere. You must take your time. You must compare prices.

Henry also informed her that he had got into the antiques business in exactly the same way, by helping out in a friend's shop. They then said goodbye to one another, Linda asking Henry to come and see her in Munich some time.

Words

loads of – (informal) a large amount of, a lot of; *stuff* – (informal) things or goods; *scales* /skeɪlz/ – instrument for measuring the weight of something; *silver-plated* – covered with a thin outer surface or layer of silver; *change* (n) – money in coins (and notes) of low value; money in small(er) units; *go down* – lower (a price).

*The Markets of London

"London is a market town. It started as a trading post, built by the Romans at the lowest point where they could cross the River Thames. Its position as a sea port and river crossing has enabled London to grow into one of the world's great cities. Markets are and always will be its lifeblood . . . .

No other city can match the number and variety of London's markets . . . . The sprawling urban mass we call London is a collection of many towns and villages, posh and poor. Each has its own marketplace which betrays the local character, heart on sleeve.

Markets provide vitality, fun and good value . . . . When so much has been swept away by bombs and planners, markets, like pubs, continue old traditions and keep communities together . . . . Despite the emergence of supermarkets and multiple chain stores, Londoners still love to shop in markets, and while some of the famous nineteenth-century street markets have dwindled or been extinguished by redevelopment, new markets have sprung up to replace them . . . . Others have been boosted by Asian, Caribbean and Middle Eastern immigrants for whom the street market is the nearest thing to their native bazaars . . . . To find out what London is like, go to its markets."

(From: Alec Forshaw and Theo Bergström, *The Markets of London*. Penguin Books. London 1986, p. 7.)

Words

lifeblood – blood regarded as the life-giving force; something which gives power and vitality; *sprawl* – (here) extend irregularly in all directions; *urban* – of a town or city; *posh* – (informal) fine, splendid, upper-class; *betray* – make known something secret; *heart on sleeve* – we talk of "wearing one's heart on one's sleeve", which means showing one's real feelings openly. The authors think that the marketplaces show you the real character of a locality; *emergence* – the appearance of supermarkets etc.; *multiple chain store* – a (usually large) shop with many branches; *redevelopment* – pulling down old buildings and replacing them with new ones; *spring up* – come into being suddenly, arise quickly; *boost* – give a push to something, give encouragement or help.

Questions

6. In what sense can the markets be said to be London's lifeblood?
7. In the author's eyes both markets and pubs offer a valuable service to a local community. What do they do?

C

Focus on language: the Present Perfect Tense

The Present Perfect is probably the most difficult tense for a foreign speaker of English to master because it is neither past nor present but looks in both directions. With the Present Perfect there is always some connection with **now**.

So let's just briefly recapitulate some of the main points about the Present Perfect.

We use the Present Perfect Tense in English to describe
(a) events which have taken place **at some time between the past and now:**

> Dover **has seen** a lot of changes over the centuries.   (up to the time Linda and Charles Willet are talking).
> John **has seen** a lot of change take place on the River Thames.   (in his experience till now)

(b) events or states which tell us about the **position now:**

> Up to now the shipping operators **have managed** to keep pace with the changing demand.   (so there's no real need for a Channel Tunnel now)
> The Castle **has been** part of my life for 60 years.   (and still is)

(c) actions and states which **began at some time in the past and are still continuing now:**

> **They have been talking** about building a Channel Tunnel for nearly 200 years.   (and they're still talking about it now)
> How long **have you been doing** this, John?   (Linda's asking him about the work he is still doing now)

Because of this connection with "now", typical adverbials used with the Present Perfect are: up to now, up to the present, so far, lately, ever, never, not yet, since (point of time) and for (period of time).

Remember that we use the **Past Tense** in English when we are talking about things that **happened at a definite time in the past.**

Exercises

1. Please put the verbs into the correct tense, Present Perfect or Past.

    a) A surge tide … a disaster along the east coast of England in 1953. (cause)
    b) Surge tides … a lot of damage right up to the present day. (cause)
    c) Her Majesty the Queen … the Thames Barrier on 8th May, 1984. (inaugurate)
    d) The Great Fire of 1666 … the whole of central London. (devastate)
    e) So far the City of London … to keep its edge over its competitors. (manage)
    f) Some street markets …, but others … to take their place. (disappear, spring up)
    g) Many of London's street markets … during the nineteenth century. (originate)
    h) Its position as a sea port and river crossing … London to grow into one of the world's great cities. (enable)

2. Please insert "since" or "for", whichever is correct.

    a) I haven't seen Linda … weeks now.
    b) Henry Gregory hasn't visited her in Munich … 1972.
    c) I've been learning English with Telekolleg … more than 3 years now.
    d) There hasn't been a really dangerous surge tide … 1953.
    e) A lot of immigrants have arrived in London … the end of the last war.
    f) He hasn't had the opportunity to practise his Spanish … the last ten years.
    g) What have you been doing … I last saw you?
    h) … when have you been waiting here?

3. Please translate into German as literally as possible and as freely as necessary.

    London could never have developed into the important town it has in fact become without the Thames. We should never forget that the main reason a town grew up here in the first place was because it was possible to build both a bridge and a port at this point on the River Thames. The bridge shortened distances for land travel and meant that in time London inevitably became the centre of an extensive road network; the port improved connections with the countries across the Channel and made it possible for ships to enter and leave with the tides.

The British press
Sports

Unit 29

A

British newspapers

A day in the life of the Gambols

Newspapers play an important role in the everyday lives of British families. If you have been to London, you must have been impressed by the great number of papers sold at every corner. More than **30 million copies** of newspapers are printed in Britain every day, the dailies and evening papers taking the greatest share. In fact, Britain has to import 75% of the paper needed for newsprint only. On Sundays more than 17 million national papers are sold. There are also up to 7000 different **periodicals and weeklies**. They sell to women (*Woman, Woman's Own*), readers with political interests (*The Observer, New Statesman*), and to groups of readers with diverse hobbies. If you are looking for general interest articles on science or sociology, you will find comprehensible and reliable information in the *New Scientist* and in *New Society*.

Many papers are proud of their long traditions and their political affiliations. What the British read will tell you a lot about their social standing, their political leanings, and their special interests. Depending on their different styles and readerships, the dailies are divided into either **"quality"** (papers) or **"popular"** (tabloids).

New capitalist owners and modern **computer technologies** have brought about changes in Fleet Street, the traditional centre of the press in London. The journalists are getting used to the new techniques, but very many printers have lost their highly qualified jobs. However, not even television has pushed aside the printed media. Watching TV and reading papers continue to be the most favourite activities in British homes.

Words

share (n) – part; *newsprint* – cheap kind of paper used mostly for newspapers; *periodical* – magazine; *diverse* – different, various; *comprehensible* – that can be understood; *reliable* – dependable, fit to be trusted; *affiliation* – connection, relationship; *leaning* – feeling or opinion (in favour of); *tabloid* – half the size format of a regular newspaper.

Questions
1. What types of papers are there in Britain, and what would be some corresponding examples in West Germany?
2. What are some of the effects of new technologies in the press?

Contents of the documentary film, part A

We meet Linda at one of the typical London newsstands run by a friendly old newsvendor. He kindly explains the different types of dailies he sells and mentions *The Daily Telegraph, The Guardian, The Times*, and the *Financial Times*. He could have added *The Independent* which has been on the market since 1986. The newsvendor, of course, mentions national dailies only and leaves out the huge number of periodicals. However, Linda, as a good American, decides to buy *Newsweek*, an American periodical.

At *The Guardian* Building Linda has an appointment with Mr Preston, the editor-in-chief of one of the more prestigious dailies. He tells Linda about the different kinds of news and topics covered in his paper. In characterizing *The Guardian* the editor emphasizes "honest reporting", a "broad sense of politics", and a journalist ethos that is committed to the reporters' conscience only. It seems that the paper's economic setup allows for this kind of freedom of the press. In Mr Preston's view this is *The Guardian's* tradition:

> "*The Guardian* has been owned for 50 years now by a trust, which is devoted purely, basically, to the continuance of *The Guardian*. And it allows the journalists who work for *The Guardian* to get on and form their own views and write their own thing.
> We do very much believe and the people who own us – and I am one of them whilst I'm editor – believe that the tradition of the paper is to allow journalists to write and report according to their conscience rather than according to what the proprietor says when he picks up the telephone."

To round off her view of the British press, Linda talks to Tony Orford, a member of the National Graphical Association, which is a big printers' union. They discuss the rapid changes in the printing industry which are taking the jobs of two thirds of all printers. Here is what this union man remarks as they pass the tomb of Karl Marx in Highgate Cemetery:

> "Karl Marx, of course, thought the workers should change the world, but we workers are finding that the world is forcing change upon us.
> … as each newspaper goes to new technology, about two thirds of the workers are losing their jobs.
> It's very difficult because most of them have spent all their working lives in the one job. And, since they have no training for anything else – they've been all their lives in printing – they face a very difficult future. It's pretty bleak.
> And the sort of payments that are made to them when they lose their jobs is only sufficient to last them for a very short time."

Words

newsvendor – a person who sells newspapers; *appointment* – a meeting at an agreed time and place; *editor-in-chief* – main editor, responsible for the contents of a newspaper; *prestigious* /preˈstɪdʒəs/ – having or bringing respect; *ethos* /ˈiːθɒs/ – set of beliefs; *commit to* – promise oneself to one position; *conscience* /ˈkɒnʃəns/ – an inner sense that judges one's actions; *setup* – organization; *devoted to* – loyal; *basically* – with regard to what is most important; *according to* – in a way that agrees with; *proprietor* – owner; *bleak* – cheerless, cold; *sufficient* – enough.

Questions

3. What are the differences between a popular (tabloid) and a quality (paper)?
4. What makes a good newspaper? Compare what the newsvendor and Mr Preston have to say.

*More about the British press

Newspapers in elections

In the 1987 election again, most dailies supported Mrs Thatcher, the conservative candidate for the office of prime minister. Of course, newspapers cannot persuade their readers to vote for a certain party. But the information presented as well as the information neglected may influence voters in an election. Here is an analysis of the 1983 election and of the role of the press in that election:

"The Conservative ownership of newspapers undoubtedly heavily influenced the election coverage in 1983, when the Press was more right-wing than at any time since the Second World War. The Tory bias was most naked in the popular Press. Lord Matthews' *Express* in its final leader concluded: 'We stand four-square and 100 per cent behind Mrs Thatcher.' His *Star*, having promised to report the election news straight, ended with a front-page splash: 'Sorry Michael, we can't vote for you.' The *Daily Mail*, influenced more by its editor English than its owner Rothermere, decided that 'by the end of Mrs Thatcher's second term there will be a new spirit, new confidence and a new prosperity'. Lord Hartwell's *Telegraph* as usual supported the Tories, only asking that Mrs Thatcher should change her attitude on unemployment. *The Times*, with a Conservative editor and owner, was equally predictable. The *Daily Mirror*, the traditional Socialist stalwart, had its doubts about the Labour manifesto, but eventually came down as the only pro-Labour paper, on the grounds that Labour was the only party that offers a realistic programme to reduce unemployment. *The Guardian* was the only daily paper sympathetic to the Alliance, and advised its readers to vote tactically against the Tories. The *Financial Times*, which had been noticeably uncommitted in its political attitudes, and showed signs of leaning towards the Alliance, was hit by a printers' strike during the campaign."

(From: A. Sampson, *The Changing Anatomy of Britain*. Coronet/Hodder & Stoughton. London 1983, pp. 437-438.)

Words

coverage – reporting; *bias* – leaning; *leader* – article expressing opinion (of editor); *Michael* – Michael Foot, Labour opposition leader; *predictable* – that can be expected; *stalwart* /ˈstɔːlwət/ – supporter of a political party; *uncommitted* – neutral.

Question

5. Which parties are mentioned, and which papers did *not* support the Conservatives?

The local press
So far we have been concerned with the national press based in London mainly. But there are local and regional papers in Britain as well.

Almost everyone reads a local or regional paper at one time or another. There are over 1,000 paid-for titles in Britain with a total readership of 55 million; they include 953 local weeklies, 67 regional evenings, 17 regional mornings and six regional Sundays. These have now been joined by more than 700 free weekly newspapers.

Three out of four people in Britain read free papers, the same number of people as read a national daily. In the south east, the proportion is higher, with 85 per cent of the population reading a freesheet. Publishers of paid-for weeklies point out that readership figures don't tell the whole story. They claim that people spend more time reading paid-for papers than free newspapers. Research by Marplan in 1985 shows that time spent reading frees was significantly less than that spent on equivalent paid-for weeklies. The Association of Free Newspapers says that the average time people spend reading a free newspaper is 25 minutes (compared with 35 minutes for a paid-for newspaper). Readers refer twice to free newspapers, on average – about the same as evening papers.

Free newspapers are the fastest growing area of the press. In the third quarter of last year, they earned £75 million – nearly 19 per cent up on 1985. Paid-for weeklies earned £59 million, an increase of 4 per cent over 1985. Put together, paid-for and free weekly papers now earn more advertising revenue than regional dailies. The local and regional press also outperform Fleet Street. In the third quarter of last year, they took £816 million in advertising revenue, compared with the nationals' earnings of £611 million. Only television gets more advertising than the non-national press.

(From: *New Society*, February 13, 1987, p. 18)

Words

title – press publication; *freesheet* – paper not paid for; *Marplan* – agency doing surveys (Umfragen); *revenue* – income; *outperform* – do better than.

Question

6. What are the main functions of "free papers"? Compare with similar papers in your home town.

B
Cricket and other sports

Golf has a wide appeal in the U.K.

Not even in England is sport the favourite **leisure** activity. When British men were asked about their activities outside their home, two thirds said they go to pubs "etc", and only one third took part in sports frequently.

When asked about their general interest in types of sports, most of them ranked football first. Cricket and golf only take a middle position, and can therefore be compared to tennis. Only small numbers of people actually take part in these sports. This seems equally true for golf, cricket and football. However, many more people go to football matches than to cricket games or golf competitions. Therefore, as **spectator sports**, football still draws the greatest crowds.

Cricket, though not as popular as football, has been called the English **"national" game**. It is the chief summer game for boys in many schools. There are a few teams of women and girls as well. In cricket two teams play on a mown grass field. The aim is for one team to score a large number of runs by hitting the ball thrown to them by the other team. This team, the "fielders", try to send the batsman out of the game as quickly as possible.

Cricket was revived in the 1970s when cup matches were introduced in England. From that time on amateur clubs were founded all over the country. International competitions have also attracted many people. In these matches teams from many **Commonwealth** nations take part with the exception of South Africa. Their team has been excluded because of the government's racist policies.

Words

leisure /ˈleʒə/ – free time; *competition* – meeting to test (sports) skills; *spectator* – a person who watches sport or another event; *score* (v) – make points in a game; *batsman* – player who strikes the ball (with a wooden "bat").

Question

7. What is the difference between spectator sports and participant sports? Give examples.

Contents of the documentary film, part B

In this film Linda gets impressions of two British sports activities when she visits one cricket club and one golf club. At the West Indian Cricket Club of Birmingham she watches a match and is puzzled by the complex rules of the game. It is the first real live match she has ever seen. Therefore she does not even try to understand what's going on.

Instead, she tries to find out about cricket as a national sport of the British. Here are some of her questions to Francis, the secretary of the club:

Linda:	Would you say that cricket is becoming more of a national sport than football?
Francis:	Yes, it's certainly a more national game than football.
Linda:	How many amateur teams would you say there are in Britain?
Francis:	Around 130, 140 within the local leagues.
Linda:	Do you think that the amateurs are bringing the level of the English game up?
Francis:	Yes, they're emulating their professionals. They're getting better, I think, at this moment.
Linda:	The Commonwealth countries are now outdoing the mother country?
Francis:	That's right, That's cricket.

At Whitby Golf Club Linda is then introduced to golf. From what she learns there, golf is a more difficult but less exclusive sport than she had expected. Linda's questions focus on the rules of the club life more than on the rules of the game.

Here is what she finds out in her talk to Alan, one of the leading members of the club:

Linda:	Alan, how old is Whitby Golf Club?
Alan:	It's ninety-odd years old. It started about 1892.
Linda:	How many members do you have?
Alan:	It's about 300 or 400 full gentlemen members, 90 ladies, and about 100 juniors.
Linda:	And from what professional backgrounds do they come?
Alan:	Oh, from every background.
Linda:	And what about the membership fees?
Alan:	For a gentleman for twelve months it's about £141, for a lady about £110, and juniors between £26 and £75 depending on their age.

When Linda herself wants to try it out, the golf instructor is happy to give her some advice. But she misses the ball and decides that golf may not be as easy as it looks.

Words

emulate – try to do as well or better than; *outdo* – do more or better than; *focus* (v) – concentrate.

Question

8. From what you learn about cricket and golf in this film, what different impressions do you get about them?

* White crowds versus black athletes

Even in cricket, some spectators seem to lose their control sometimes. Such an incident is discussed in the two following text excerpts, one from a leader and the other from a letter to the editor.

A vicious virus in cricket

Racial abuse against black athletes by white sports crowds is not new. But it does seem to be on the increase. So far, inevitably, football crowds are the worst and most persistent offenders, especially at some London grounds. Cricket, though, has managed to avoid providing an arena for such boorishness, albeit probably more by luck than judgment. Cricket crowds, however, are changing. Last Sunday, during a (…) game at Weston-super-Mare between Somerset and Worcestershire, the West Indies' captain, Mr Viv Richards, was so provoked by yobbish chants of "black bastard" that he marched into the crowd to confront his abusers. Mr Richards's action was highly effective (as most of his actions are) and, happily, was warmly approved by most of the crowd. But the incident was a warning. When the greatest batsman of the age, the noblest sight that the game has to offer, is treated in this way – and when, unusually for such a restrained man, he responds – then the cricket authorities need to beware that the enemy is already inside the door.

(…)

The real problem is cultural. It is to persuade young, white, working-class men that society is not indifferent to racial abuse. That means hard work. It means having nerves that are jangled by such behaviour. It means having a smart response to outbreaks. It means setting a good example. The one thing it does not mean is pretending the problem doesn't exist. Somerset cricket has a lesson for English sport as a whole.

(From: *The Guardian*, August 6, 1968, p. 8.)

Words

vicious /ˈvɪʃəs/ – evil, dangerous; *abuse* (v) – saying unjust things; *persistent* – happening again and again; *offender* – person who does wrong; *boorish* – behaving rough, ill-mannered; *albeit* /ɔːlˈbiːɪt/ – though; *yobbish* – behaving in an ill-mannered way; *approve* – welcome; *restrained* – holding back, keeping oneself under control; *jangle* (v) – irritate very much; *pretend* – say falsely.

Letter to the editor

Sir,
I wonder what evidence you have for suggesting (Leader, August 6) that racial abuse at cricket matches is on the increase. In my unpleasant experience it has been consistently noticeable for a few years now. Only two or three summers ago I had the misfortune to witness one of the greatest fast bowlers in the world, Andy Roberts, being pelted with bananas as he walked out to bat in a cup competition for Leicestershire at Northampton. The incident was greeted with general hilarity. All around me young children looked up at their fathers rocking with laughter and laughed too. And so in an instance the die is cast for another generation of blinkered unquestioning racism.

All of this happened in an area right under the pavilion and players' balcony. (…) However, what was most noticeable about the Roberts incident was the virtual non-existence of any protest, and that's why I treat with scepticism your account of the Weston-super-Mare crowd warmly applauding Viv Richards as the great man waded in to sort out the trouble. I wonder how many of them were prepared to do the same.

Let's explode this myth about cricket being relatively free of such disturbances, shall we? Lots of people are racialist inside cricket grounds because lots of people are racialist outside cricket grounds as well. The safety in numbers aspect of spectator sport gives them an excellent platform for their odious views. As an anti-racist at such events I personally have *never* found myself in the majority.

Yours faithfully,
Robert Chapman.

(From: *The Guardian*, August 8, 1986, p. 21.)

Words

evidence – proof; *pelt* (v) – attack by throwing things; *hilarity* – loud laughter; *the die is cast* (proverb) – the course is set and cannot be changed; *blinkered* – with blinders (Scheuklappen) on, blind; *virtual* – total; *account* (n) – report; *wade in* – walk in; *explode* – destroy, show the falsity of.

Questions

9. Explain this phrase in the leader: "the enemy is inside the door".
10. Why does the first sentence of the letter to the editor seem misleading at first sight?

C

Focus on language: Dependent clauses

Dependent clauses (i.e. relative clauses, nominal clauses, temporal clauses, purpose clauses, reason clauses, etc.) are used if you want to move on from simple to complex sentences. Dependent clauses cannot stand on their own, but depend on main clauses – or on other dependent clauses – and refer to one word usually. Quite often this word will be either a noun or a verb.

– Complex sentence structures can indeed be very complex. This is often the case when more than one dependent clause is involved. Sentences with many dependent clauses can often be found in spoken speech. Ideas tend to become more complex in a speaker's mind while he or she is expressing these ideas in sentences (cf exercise 1).

- Among the most common dependent clauses are relative clauses. They refer back to a noun or pronoun and give more information about it. Relative clauses start with **who** for persons and **which** for objects. **That** can be used to refer to both objects and persons:

    The *people* **who** own us believe (in freedom of the press).
    The Guardian has been owned by a *trust* **which** is devoted to the continuance of the paper.
    We try to cover *issues* **that** other papers don't get into.
    The *printers* **that** have no training for anything else face a very difficult future.

- Another frequently used group of dependent clauses are nominal clauses. They are sometimes called "that-clauses" too. All nominal clauses take the place of nouns in a sentence, often that of the direct object:

    We know (**what?**) – that newspapers are faced with hard times.

- Sometimes, especially in informal speech, the conjunction "that" is dropped in nominal clauses:

    Marx thought (**that**) the workers should change the world.

Exercises

1. Here is one long complex sentence from the interview with the editor-in-chief of *The Guardian*. And this is what you can do to analyse the sentence: a) Fill in the conjunctions and relative pronouns left out (do *not* look at the complete version on p.29). b) Underline the dependent clauses. How many can you find, and what types of dependent clauses are they? c) Which is the first and the last word of the main clause?

    We do very much believe ... the people ... own us – ... I am one of them ... I'm editor – believe ... the tradition of the paper is to allow journalists to write and report according to their conscience rather than to ... the proprietor says ... he picks up the telephone.

2. Here is a list of simple clauses. Arrange them into meaningful combinations of main and dependent clause. Use the best suitable conjunction or relative pronoun. In the end, there should be six complex sentences.

    a) In 1975 the Sportsman of the Year was a cricketer.
    b) Its use in the provincial press is more widespread.
    c) No Commonwealth countries play cricket against South Africa.
    d) *Today* is a new national newspaper.
    e) More than 70 newspapers and magazines are produced by members of ethnic minorities.
    f) But this is not a rigid distinction.
    g) About half of the national newspapers now use some computer technology.
    h) Its government follows racialist policies.
    i) It is published seven days a week.
    j) 40 of these are printed in Asian languages.
    k) National newspapers are often thought of as either "quality" or "popular" papers.
    l) Public interest in cricket began to grow.

3. Translate the final paragraph of the letter to the editor on page 35.

Schools – old and new
The Open University

Unit 30

A

Schools in England

An English language class at Holland Park Comprehensive School

Table: 16-19 year olds in full time education by socio-economic group of father

professional	72%
employers/managers	48%
intermediate	45%
skilled manual	29%
semi and unskilled manual	27%

(From: *New Society*, February 6, 1987, p. 11.)

It is statistics like these collected only three years ago that worry many people in England, especially parents and teachers. The most obvious point seems to be that the time spent at school during adolescence still has a lot to do with the **social class** of a child's parents. In international comparison it is often pointed out that English children actually go to school for less time than children in Japan, the USA, and, perhaps, West Germany. It is this second point more than the first which unites present critics of the educational system in England even across different parties.

This deficit comes as a surprise after more than 40 years of **reform** and improvement in English schools since World War II. Today, separate secondary schools have become a thing of the past since almost all towns and regions in England have "gone comprehensive". The old "tripartite" school system used to separate children at the age of 11. After primary school the children were sent to different schools like grammar schools and secondary modern schools. These offered different school-leaving certificates, and only grammar school pupils could go on to university. Today, almost all towns have comprehensive schools instead of the traditional secondary schools.

However, with lack of money in the state school system, rich parents send their children to independent or so-called "public", i.e. **private schools**. These schools, among them such famous institutions as Eton, have a long tradition of educating the English elite. Even today, only 7% live in such boarding-schools. The remaining 93% go to the large secondary state schools for children of all abilities from a single district. These schools intend to provide a wide (**"comprehensive"**) range of education and have an intake of pupils from all social classes.

The basic battle today is no longer between comprehensive and public schools as institutions. The overriding issue is whether education should be a public service for all or a private investment for the happy few. But in each case, the English educational system is expected to raise academic standards, to conform to a national core curriculum, and to prepare kids for working life, too.

Words
professional (n) – people with an academic degree, e.g. lawyers and doctors; *skilled* – trained; *manual* – done with the hands; *adolescence* /ˈædəʊˈlesns/ – period between being a child and an adult; *deficit* /ˈdefɪsɪt/ – too low quality; *tripartite* /ˈtraɪˈpɑːtaɪt/ – having three parts; *grammar school* – mainly academic education and preparing for higher education; *secondary modern school* – offers a more technical and less academic education; *independent* – not needing other things or people; *boarding-school* – school where children live; *intake* – number entering or taken in; *overriding* – prevailing, most important; *issue* /ˈɪʃuː/ (n) – an important point; *raise* – lift; *core* – the most important or central part; *curriculum* /kəˈrɪkjʊləm/ – a course of study in a school or college.

Questions
1. Explain "comprehensive" and "public" school.
2. What would be their counterparts in West Germany, and in what way would the German school system be different from the English?

Contents of the documentary film, part A

In this film Linda is seen visiting one public and one comprehensive school. The short interview with public schoolboys, in front of Canterbury Cathedral, shows a few interesting aspects of their life. Linda learns about their school-day routine and must have been impressed by their well-balanced behaviour in public. The only inside view Linda gets is a fencing lesson. It shows the importance of traditional discipline and of elite sports.

But what really seems to strike Linda is the international intake of pupils at the school. It is fairly easy to see that most of them do not come from Canterbury. But where are they from?

"I come from East Africa, Kenya."
"And I'm from the Bahamas."
"I'm from Nigeria. (...)"
"I live locally. (...)"
"I live in Portugal."

Linda then moves on to a very different kind of school. It is Holland Park Comprehensive, one of the big schools in London. From Margaret Pringle, the headmistress, Linda learns a lot about the character and the educational ethos of this school:

"We're big – 15 hundred. We're mixed. And what I think is special about the school is that we're mixed in a number of ways. Our children come from a real mixture of backgrounds, of races, of languages. They're mixed ability. We're boys and girls. I think it's what makes it a very exciting place to work at …
(...)
I think individual schools in England have some power of deciding what their ethos is. For example whether they want a uniform or not. We've decided we don't want a uniform. We've decided we do want to put the emphasis on children's self–discipline, rather than discipline from the teachers, although, of course, that has to be an element in any school.
We put a lot of responsibility on the children for their own learning. And I think parents know that, and they know that their children will be trusted and will be expected to be treated as young adults here.
So I think when they choose us, they know that that's the background."

In other scenes Linda takes part in an English language class for immigrant pupils. They too come from all parts of the world, e.g. Morocco, Sudan and Ghana. The international background of the pupils seems to unite the comprehensive and the public school in our film. These children, however, do have language problems which require special treatment. Here is what Linda learns from Chris May, one of the teachers, about language learning problems and the teaching strategies to overcome them:

"We have some children who come to the school speaking no English really at all. And some children who've come with quite good English. But we still need to have their …, they have some problems with their written English especially.
(...)
Well, we use two things mainly (as teaching strategies). One is, we have withdrawal classes, where we take children in fairly small groups and can work at the language. And we also go into classes to help them: an extra teacher to help children who have particular problems with language."

Words
fence (v) – fight with a long thin sword as a sport; *headmistress* – female teacher in charge of a school; *emphasis* – stress, special force; *responsibility* – trustworthiness; *adult* – grown-up; *treatment* – way of dealing with; *withdrawal* – moving away.

Questions

3. What struck you about the public school children?
4. Describe the educational ethos of Holland Park Comprehensive.

*More about English schools

Money lies at the heart of the problem

Welcome to the modern-day version of England's dark, satanic mills. A hundred years after it was founded, the country's state-funded school system has never seemed in worse shape. Chronically underfunded and overlooked, the schools are facing a host of crises. Older buildings are simply crumbling away. There are acute shortages of books, equipment and furniture. Add to that poorly paid and demoralized teachers and the result is a system heading for total breakdown. In response, a growing number of parents are spending as much as $10,000 a year to put their kids in the country's elite public (actually private) schools, strengthening the trend toward a separate and unequal educational system.

(...)

It is little wonder, then, that English children have been flocking in record numbers to public schools. But the number of places available is severely limited. (At present there are roughly 500,000 students in the country's 2,000 public schools, and 7 million in the state system.) Critics contend that such a trend only aggravates the latent class differences in England, which, as they see it, is the reason for the problem in the first place. "I don't believe the English have ever had a great respect for education", says Dr. John Rae, former headmaster of Westminster, a high-ranking public school. "They're happy to kick most children out on the streets when they're 16, and send only the very brightest to universities. We're very elitist." Indeed, only about 30 percent of students from state schools actually go on to higher education.

(From: *Newsweek*, July 21, 1986, pp. 44-45.)

Words

mill – factory; *shape* – condition; *underfunded* – with not enough money; *crumble away* – break down gradually; *head for* – move towards; *flock* – go in great numbers; *contend* – argue; *elitist* /eɪˈliːtɪst/ – helping the best.

Questions

5. In what ways is money responsible for the problems in English schools?
6. Why could education in England be called "very elitist"?

A young black at school

"Here, you want a story, I'll give you a story. I went to school three years with a bunch of kids, none of 'em could read. Black kids, white kids, none of 'em could read. So they put us in this class together, man, where there was supposed to be special help for us, just in reading, you understand. We got, I don't know, maybe twenty-five kids in that room. Room used to smell too, man, 'cause it was right next to the kitchen. They used to keep all the extra tables and chairs in there, but then they cleared it out for us, all of us being the special cases.

You want to know what happens? First thing they get is a white teacher, and she ain't old, man, she's Queen Victoria's grandmother! And we're the first blacks she has ever seen in her life. But you think she says something about it? Oh no, she's real cool about it. She gives us seats where we have to sit and doesn't it come out whites over there and us over here? Okay, I can take that. I say to myself, well, she ain't going to be no close friend, man, but maybe the old lady's going to help me read. That's a joke, man. A *joke*! She has us reading books out loud, right? She makes the white kids read and they go on and on and on. Then comes us, and what does she do? She listens to us two seconds and says, 'That's wonderful, Lanny', and goes on to the next one. Two seconds later, 'That's wonderful, Snaker'. Two seconds later, 'That's wonderful, Elaine'. She never hears us for more than a minute, man. So who do you guess got anything out of that special class, man? Wasn't us, I can tell you for sure.

But now I'll tell you something about her, and this is all happening when I was nine, but I knew it then, man, we all knew it then. That woman never knew she was doing it, man. You would have asked her, maybe she'd tell you she treats us all the same but for some reason the white kids just do better than the black kids. Can't tell you why that is, but they do. Maybe it's their home life, you know. That woman never once saw what she was doing, and I'm not sure the white kids did either. But the black kids did. Fact is, *that's* what I learned in that special class. First, I learned that blacks didn't stand a chance with her so we'd none of us get to read properly, and the second thing was that you can't learn nothing in a room next to the kitchen. It smells too much, makes it so you can't think."

(From: Thomas J. Cottle, *Black Testimony*. Wildwood House Ltd. London 1978, pp. 51–53.)

30

Words
bunch – group; *clear out* – put away; *Queen Victoria* – reigned 1837-1901; *proper* – right.

Questions
7. What can you say about the person interviewed and about the language used?
8. What explanation is offered for the experience described?

B
The Open University

The OU offers its programmes and services to people of all ages and backgrounds.

The "OU", as the Open University is sometimes abbreviated, was founded 15 years ago. This experiment has served as a model for **adult and tertiary education** in other countries (e.g. the **Fernuniversität** Hagen). And the courses produced by the OU are used by many people not enrolled there. In fact, English-speaking students in Belgium can take part in the TV courses too. The Open University started as a correspondence university working with carefully designed course material and TV programmes for study at home. In contrast to the established universities the OU was intended to be **"open" in many ways**. Students do not have to live on the campus or go to classes there. They do not need formal qualifications from school and they can work for further education instead of regular degrees. Finally, most students will be older and will have some sort of previous work experience.

This way, the OU has "produced" **45000 graduates** over ten years at an average age of 38. Teachers and housewives have been among the main beneficiaries. At present, one third of the OU students are workers, and almost every second student is female. It is interesting and a remarkable achievement that the majority of OU students come from working-class families.

Words
abbreviate – make shorter; *enrol* – become officially a member of (a university, group); *correspondence (course)* – information and work are exchanged between teacher and student by post; *previous* – earlier in time; *beneficiary* /benɪˈfɪʃərɪ/ – person who receives some advantage; *achievement* – the successful gaining of something.

Questions

9. Explain "adult education", "further education" and "tertiary education" and point out the differences.
10. In what ways can the OU be considered to be "open"?

Contents of the documentary film, part B

Our film was not made at Milton Keynes, the headquarters of the Open University, but at an OU summer school held at Stirling University. The experience offered by Joe McBride and Cathie Hickman in their interviews seems quite typical of OU careers. When asked about their motivation for enrolling at the Open University, here is what they said:

Joe: ... at the time I enrolled I was employed, but I'm unemployed now. And the reason I decided to take a degree is because I have no formal qualifications, and I decided that at this time in my life it would be a good thing to get them.

Cathie: ... I'm working as a physiotherapist in Manchester at the moment. And (as) physiotherapists, we only get a diploma. We don't get a degree. So for promotion I'm doing this, for ... to get a degree.

And this is how they study:

Joe: There are two broadcasts a week on this course. One is over the weekend and one is on a Thursday morning. And I find no difficulty getting up for them. I'm prepared to make the sacrifice.

Cathie: ... the programme on the Sunday is on at 9.20, which is fine. And the problem is when you miss that, it's about 5 to 7 on Thursday, which is difficult if you've been out the night before and you've got work the next day. I just can't concentrate sometimes.

What has studying at the OU meant for both of them and for their families and friends?

Joe: Oh, it's opened a new range on life; it broadens your concepts and ideals, and makes you question situations and facts that you would have allowed to pass unnoticed before. It makes you think a little ..., it makes you use your brain a bit more.

Cathie: ... I think it's increased my confidence a lot, that I can argue ideas better with other people. That's been good.

Joe: It's more important than you think to talk over doing the course with members of your family, because they're going to be affected most.

Cathie: ... it's sometimes very difficult because friends don't understand what you're doing, so you can't talk about it to them. If you've got a good tutorial group, it helps.

Questions
11. What are some of the disadvantages of studying at the Open University?
12. In comparing Joe's and Cathie's answers to Linda's questions, what do you find?

*The Open University from within

Summer schools have been the beginning of new friendships, and have brought together unexpected people; there are not many places where you will find a peeress and a coalminer chatting entirely naturally about their common work. Of course, Open University work has sometimes put strains on family life, and the chief comment of one of the first graduates was "students need sympathetic families".

Where the husband or wife does not understand or sympathize with the other's dedication to study, it can put a serious strain upon a marriage. But others have found that it has enriched their family life. I think of some families where husband and wife are both students, and their intellectual interaction with one another in consequence. I think of the tolerant amusement of some children, one of whom remarked "Mummy, that university is sending you silly. All you say is 'uum'", and another of whom looks forward to the arrival of philosophy units illustrated by cartoons so that she can look at "Mummy's comic strip".

I think of a mother whose daughter left school without a needed A-level in English. The daughter was shy about going to evening classes on her own, so her mother, a delightful extrovert, bubbling over with joy, said "I'll come along with you, ducks; it'll be a bit of fun". The daughter got her grade E pass; the mother got an A and thought "What a lark! What about this Open University thing?" and is now with the admiration and enthusiasm of her family delightedly moving through a degree programme with excellent grades. And I think of a woman with seven children under 12, whose Open University work has made a united family still more united, and whose husband, whose parents and whose husband's parents have all been sharing in the care of the children during her summer schools and other absences.

Three comments from students may round off this picture. The first from a police-constable: "The work is exhilarating, but also exhausting." The second from a housewife: "Knowledge is so much of life." The third from a secretary: "It messes up your whole life – but it's worth it."

(From: R. Bivand, *Britain. Continuity and Change.* Simon and Schuster. Hertfordshire/England. Originally: Pergamon. Kronberg 1981, pp. 87-88.)

Words

peeress – female member of noble rank (baron, etc.); *chat* (v) – talk in a friendly informal way; *strain* (n) – state of tension; *dedication* – being very interested; *A-level (Advanced Level)* – higher examination taken at 17, standard for entrance to university; *extrovert* (n) – person who likes to spend time with other people; *lark* (n) – amusement, bit of fun; *admiration* – feeling of pleasure and respect; *absence* – state of being away; *constable* /ˈkʌnstəbl/ – policeman of the lowest rank; *exhilarate* /ɪgˈzɪləreɪt/ – make cheerful and excited; *exhaust* /ɪgˈzɔːst/ – tire out.

Question
13. Why are "sympathetic families" so important for Open University students?

C
Focus on language: the Simple Present Tense

Constructing the Simple Present Tense of a verb is not difficult in English. But the problem is when to use Simple Present and when not.

– In contrast to the Simple Present, the Present Progressive is used to tell us what's going on (at present):

> She **is working** *at the moment*.

The Simple Present is used to tell us what it's like:

> He **works** from 8 to 4 *every day*.

– Simple Present focusses on facts and qualities rather than on actions and processes. Therefore the Simple Present Tense is used to describe objects:

> That one **looks** like a *house*.

– But it can also describe conditions:

> *Studying* at the Open University **opens** your concepts and ideas.

– The Simple Present can finally describe routines:

> I just **can't concentrate** *sometimes*.

Exercises

1. Change the quotations of the contents of part B from direct into indirect speech (from "Oh, it's opened ..." until "... it helps", p.43). Imagine that Linda is telling TELEKOLLEG students in Germany about what studying at the OU means for Cathie and Joe. Remember that the pronouns must be changed (e.g. "I" to "she") and that the tenses must be backshifted (e.g. Present Perfect to Past Perfect).

2. Reconstruct the following text about the Open University. The blanks ask for verb constructions only three of which are not in the Simple Present. There are, however, two negations and five passive voice constructions. Here is a list of the verbs to be used: *be, be, come, come together, concentrate, give, include, live, range, recommend, sell, send, study, transmit, use*
   a) Open University degree students ... adults over 21, who ... at home and ... in their spare time.
   b) They ... from many different walks of life and ... from a RAF pilot to a miller.
   c) Past graduates ... a former Chancellor of the University and an 81-year-old grandmother.
   d) Staff and students ... on a campus, instead specially produced materials ... direct to students' homes, TV programmes ... by the BBC, and personal tuition ... at local study centres.
   e) The University ... exclusively on degrees, and since 1978 the fastest growing work ... continuing education.
   f) The teaching materials ... in other British universities, and the correspondence texts ... through bookshops often.
   g) Many schools and colleges ... the OU radio and TV programmes to their students.

3. Translate the second paragraph of the text on p. 40, starting from "It is little wonder ..." to the end.

Birmingham and its multi-racial society — Unit 31

A
Birmingham – workshop of the world 🎧

A Birmingham canal barge

"Since Birmingham cannot be removed to the sea, the sea must be brought to Birmingham."

Did you know that the Birmingham area has more miles of canals than Venice? Of course, these canals in and around Birmingham have served different purposes and are a lot younger than those of Venice. These waterways were constructed at a time when Birmingham was on its way to becoming the "workshop of the world", one of the first world centres of industrial production. Within five years only – during the so-called canal-mania of 1789-1793 – Birmingham had become the centre of almost the entire **British canal network**.

Transport has always been important in the development of industrial production because raw materials had to be shipped to the places of production, and the products had to be distributed to the customers. And before the coming of the railways – which was around 1840 – waterways provided the only means of **transporting heavy goods**.

Canals not only connected Birmingham with the seaports like Liverpool. Many small canals also served to link coal pits and factories. The population of Birmingham was growing rapidly. New houses and churches were built, and the town centre was crowded with **workshops** and houses.

After gas lighting had been invented, many **brass tubes** and other metal parts were needed. In Birmingham many workers turned to making these items. Then, many towns and houses put in water pipes, too. From the 1830s, machines were used to draw out the tubes, and far more could be made more quickly.

In Birmingham today, industry is still important, but the canals have lost their original function. Transport by road and rail has become much more important than canal freight. Yet the canal system is useful even today. Canals supply water for industrial production, and they also drain the water after rains. In addition, the canals are being used for **recreation** and for tours into the city's past. That is why even today the city council is putting money into the old canal system restoring and conserving as many parts of it as possible.

Words
purpose – intention or plan; *construct* – build; *mania* – strong unreasonable desire; *distribute* – deliver, bring to; *connect* – link; *brass* – hard yellow metal; *tube* – pipe; *item* – piece; *drain* (v) – cause water to flow off; *recreation* – way of spending free time.

Questions
1. In which two ways are industrialization and transport connected?
2. How has transport changed from 1800 to the present?

Contents of the documentary film, part A

At the beginning of this programme we listen to a song. *Dirty Old Town* is a well-known folk song, not referring to the city of Birmingham only. But the setting of the song and the atmosphere described make it a very suitable introduction to Birmingham and Birmingham's past.
This song, written by Ewan McColl and presented by Alex Campbell in the film, is heard in many different versions around the world. Here is what seems to be Alex Campbell's "personal" version:

> I met my love by the gasworks wall,
> Dreamed a dream by the old canal.
> I kissed my girl by the factory wall.
>   Dirty old town,
>   dirty old town.
>
> Clouds are drifting across the moon.
> Cats are prowling on their beat.
> Spring's a girl from the streets at night.
>   Dirty old town,
>   dirty old town.
>
> I heard a siren from the docks,
> Saw a train set the night on fire.
> Her smile's the spring on the smokey wind.
>   Dirty old town,
>   dirty old town.

> I'm gonna make me a big sharp axe,
> shining steel tempered in the fire.
> I'll chop you down like an old dead tree.
>> Dirty old town,
>> dirty old town.

This song is certainly a very private, personal account of a "dirty old town". And it is not easy to understand, especially if you look at its surprising turn in the final verse.
As the song fades away, we watch Linda taking her tour of the Birmingham canals. She is accompanied by Andrew Blizzard. At the end of the programme we learn that he has a degree from the Open University and works for the Local History Department of the City of Birmingham. One of his jobs seem to be guided tours of the town and its history. Canals offer interesting and sometimes nostalgic views of this town's industrial quarters.
Here are some of Andrew's comments as they glide along on the canal barge:

> "Well, we're on the main Birmingham-to-Wolverhampton canal, which was the first one opened within the network of canals in Birmingham and the West Midlands. I think it opened in 1769. And at that time, the Industrial Revolution period, there was a lot of industry and a great expanse of industry of all kinds related to coal and iron and metal-working.
> Many of the factories and warehouses are in a derelict state, but of course some years ago they were heavily used by a variety of industries. However, we have seen one or two factories that actually are being used now by firms making perhaps sort of light ..., you know, for light industry within Birmingham and the West Midlands.
> Nowadays, well, the canals are used for recreational purposes. You know, for school party trips or office outings going into perhaps the countryside towards Worcestershire or coming on an industrial tour like this one."

Words
prowl – move about silently; *temper* (v) – bring metal to firmness; *expanse* – wide space, great amount; *relate to* – connect to; *derelict* – left to decay; *outing* – a short pleasure trip.

Question
3. How would you describe the mood evoked in the song *Dirty Old Town*?

*Birmingham a century ago

By 1870, there were over 240,000 people living in Birmingham. Most of these people were working in small workshops. There must have been at least 7000 of them in all, most of them in converted private houses.
Working conditions used to be very bad. Rooms were overcrowded, and full of fumes dangerous to health. Brassworkers in particular worked in bad conditions and many of them died young. There were many boys and girls, some of them as young as 6 years of age. They worked the same hours as

the men – that is about twelve hours a day for six days in the week. Women were especially employed in the explosives works and in the pin and button industries.

Here is a report about working conditions in Birmingham just before the turn of the century. It was published by a magazine under the title of *Child-Slaves of Britain*.

"For the sheer misery ... of laborious and underpaid labour in which children are forced to participate as long as their little fingers can move and their eyes keep open, it is in the kitchens of the squalid homes in the courts and closes that we must look. There are a number of trades in Birmingham for which the home-labour of women and children is employed. Finding one's cotton, hemp and needles, twopence an hour may be earned by a woman assisted by one or two children in sewing the chains on to the leather for soldiers' chin-straps. But here child labour almost always fails. Government is very particular, and any strap which as to its seventy-two links (four stitches to each link) is not sewn in the best style of sempstress-ship is pitilessly refused. Deducting expenses, and allowing for goods refused, 1*s* 8*d* has been earned in 2½ days by two people working for Government from 6 a.m. to 11 p.m. Where firemen's chin-straps have to be made, the needle has to be pushed through four thicknesses of leather. It is hard work for little hands.

At wrapping up hairpins in paper, ten to the paper, with one outside to hold the package together, a light employment in which any member of the family circle may engage, as much as 2¼*d* may be earned by two people, or four children, in a couple of days. For this sum 1000 packages have to be made up. The goods must be fetched from the factory and carried back there besides.

One penny a day can be gained by a child in bending the tin clasp round safety-pins – "bending safety-pins" they call it. The nimble fingers of children are apt at this work. The payment is at the rate of halfpenny a gross, but for some varieties of safety-pins as much as twopence for three gross is cheerfully paid by the manufacturers. So terrible is the competition by children in this trade that, as an old woman of ninety told me in a house "back of Unit Street", when her husband was alive they could, by working all the week – he from 5 a.m. till 11 p.m., and she from 9 a.m. till the same hour at night – earn two shillings a week between them."

(From: P. Keating, ed., *Into Unknown England*, 1866-1913. Fontana/Collins. Glasgow 1976, pp. 185-186.)

Words
convert /kənˈvɜːt/ (v) – change; *fume* (n) – strong-smelling gas; *laborious* – hard, not easy; *squalid* – dirty; *hemp* – German: Hanf; *sempstress* (= seamstress) – woman who makes a living by sewing; *deduct* – take off; *1s 8d* = 1 shilling 8 pence; *clasp* (n) – German: Klammer; *nimble* – quick-moving; *apt* – suitable, well-suited; *gross* – twelve dozen.

Questions
4. What kinds of jobs did children have to do and what could they earn?
5. How does the writer view the working conditions described?

B
Birmingham – multicultural city ∞

Mounted policeman

After looking at Birmingham's past we now turn to the town's present situation. How do you like such **exotic views** of England: a mosque, shops with foreign-language signs, and people from Asia and the Caribbean? Many German tourists are, indeed, surprised by the many different, non-European faces they see when they come to London. But most of us will also have heard of riots in the inner cities of London, Liverpool and Birmingham. These violent clashes between the police and immigrant groups, so-called race riots, keep turning up in the news about the United Kingdom. Like many of the foreign workers in West Germany, many West-Africans and Asians in the U.K. suffer from **discrimination** in various sectors of life, e.g. at school and on the job. But unlike migrant workers in West Germany, almost all of these people from Jamaica or Pakistan are British citizens legally. Being treated as second-class citizens must be painful, especially for those younger people of the second generation who were born in the U.K. and have no connection with the faraway countries their parents came from.

Violence involving West-Africans and Pakistanis is usually *not* caused by these people and certainly not by the different colour of their skin or their different cultural practices. The real roots of **riots** are social: high unemployment among young blacks, bad housing, general poverty. But the police themselves seem to play a key role in such unrest. In tense situations the police may be unable to control the violence and may even contribute to an escalation.

Civil rights groups in the U.K., both black and white, have criticized the **police** for their behaviour in riots. Others, however, are asking for more power and more weapons for the police in order to be able to control such situations. The experience of many riots indicates that this may be a dangerous route to follow. Sometimes the mere presence of police forces encourages young people to express their feelings of frustration and anger.

Therefore the police and some politicians have started to rethink policing methods. In Birmingham, for instance, the police are trying to recruit new officers from the ethnic communities. This way they hope to build up confidence between the police authorities and the communities in troubled areas. But stereotypes on both sides have made this a very difficult and long-term project.

Words

riot (n) – violent actions of group in a public place; *citizen* – member of a particular country; *escalation* – getting more serious and spreading out.

Questions

6. What are some of the underlying causes of riots?
7. Describe the dilemma of police forces in a riot.

Contents of the documentary film, part B

The film is concerned with different aspects of policing, especially with the modern computer equipment of the Birmingham police and with problems of intercultural conflict and cooperation. Linda is first introduced to the Computer and Control Room of the **Bournville Police Station** in Birmingham. Superintendent Jim Arthur explains to her that all police calls from in and around Birmingham are collected here. Computers are used to assist the police in reacting quickly to different demands:

> "Now this is a typical console of the Control Room. (…) Any call that comes in from West Midlands County, an emergency or a normal call, telephone call, will come into this room. And from this room we are linked directly to the commander control computer, which is in fact in the basement of this building."

The phone call that Linda witnesses is not serious. But it shows that even minor problems, like the Muezzin's call for prayer, may cause irritation among the white population. Here is how the operator handles this telephone call:

> "West Midlands Police emergency …
> And your name, sir? …
> Mr Evans …
> And your address? …
> 21 Belgrave Road …
> And what's the problem? …
> So it's excessive noise … from the mosque.
> All right, Mr Evans, I'll get someone down there."

Later, at the Birmingham Central Mosque, Linda is introduced to the secretary of the religious community. He is full of praise for the cooperation with the police, but gives no details:

> "So I'll ... I will say that the police authorities, when we call them in such problems, they come over.
> They sit with us.
> They solve our problems.
> They make good relations with us.
> And I appreciate them, that ... thankful to them.
> They are dealing with us in a very nice way."

Back at the police station, Superintendent Jim Swingewood tells Linda about police routines. Linda wants to know about how police horses react in riots and learns that they are very well trained and are not more difficult to deal with than the people.

Here is what the police officer has to say about intercultural conflicts in Birmingham:

> "There are many hundreds of different and difficult situations we have with our cultural problems here in Birmingham.
> For instance, we've got the Sikh community wanting to carry daggers in public.
> That's against our law.
> We've got the problem of punishment in mosque schools. They are much harder on their children than we in Britain are."

In the long run, he continues, the almost all-white police force will have to try to integrate black policemen:

> "At present, we've got 98, which is very few, compared with 6000.
> So the difficulty is getting the black people to join our force which in some areas they believe is a very small, low job. For instance, in India and Pakistan, they think it is beneath their dignity to join the police force."

Words
console /ˈkɒnsəʊl/ (n) – flat surface on which are the controls for a machine; *excessive* – too much; *appreciate* /əˈpriːʃieɪt/ – put a high value on; *dagger* – two-edged knife used as a weapon; *dignity* – true worth.

Question
8. Which intercultural problems are mentioned and what is done by the police to solve them?

*Relations with the police – a personal view

The film presents problems between different cultural groups in the United Kingdom mainly from the point of view of the Birmingham police. To complement this "official" view, the following text offers a very different story. This time the relations with the police are seen from the other side. The incident described is taken from an oral history interview with a black British girl. It is a very personal story and does not claim to offer an objective view of the police.

"One night my boyfriend was going home from my house and it so happened that it was his birthday and I bought him an expensive razor and he had several other presents. After getting the midnight service, he was walking home on the road that he lives on. A police car drew up and they stopped him and they wanted to know where he was going. He told them he was going home. They wanted to know what he had in his hands and what he was doing on the streets so late, so he told them he was going home and the presents he had in his hands were presents from his girlfriend. But they couldn't have believed him 'cause they kept on asking him where he got it from. Eventually they took him down to the police station and he was there for three hours before they 'phoned me up and asked me had he been at my house that night and did he have anything with him when he left and I told them that I bought him a shaver.

Anyway, the next morning I saw him and the whole of his face was full with bruises and he got marks all over his body, apparently they beat him up because they didn't believe that the razor was a birthday present, they kept insisting that maybe he stole it. When he kept saying no it was a birthday present they kept hitting him. It is things like this that brings the conclusion that the police are racist. I pass people when they are being stopped by the police, I mean, I have been in a car myself and the police just stop us for no reason and they want to know all kinds of irrelevant information, like who are the rest of people in the car beside the driver and where are we going.

As far as I can see the more down and out a black man is, or the black youth is, the more advantages the police will take of you, if you happen to look dirty or scruffy, or walking around midday when you should be working the more the police harass you. I don't think they like to see black people better themselves and if they see a young youth with a car they will find excuses to stop him three and four times in one day on the pretext of just routine spot checks."

(From: D. Bishton/B. Homer, ed., *Talking Blues. Black Community speaks about its relations with the police.* AFFOR. Birmingham 1978, p. 10.)

Words

oral history – interviews with (historical) eyewitnesses; *claim* (v) – beanspruchen.

Questions

9. How can you recognize that the text was taken from an "oral", spoken interview?
10. How does the girl describe "harassing" by the police, and how does she try to explain this behaviour?

C

Focus on language: Prepositions

In general, prepositions express relations. These relations can be between things:

>He has got a unique *post* **within** the library *service*.

But persons can also be related by means of prepositions:

>*They* are dealing **with** *us* in a very nice way.

– Prepositions of place are used to indicate positions:

>The computer is **in** the *basement*.

And they are used to show directions:

>P.C. Bolton will put it **on to** the *computer*.

– Some verbs, the so-called prepositional verbs (phrasal verbs), take a specific preposition. In these cases, the verb must be learnt along with the preposition, e.g.:

    It was just a neighbour *complaining* **about** the noise.

– Many nouns, too, can go with prepositional phrases. In the following example, even two prepositional phrases follow the noun because both "noise" and "mosque" are described more closely:

    The call was complaining about *noise* **from** the *mosque* **in** Belgrave Road.

Exercises

1. In the following advertisement, published by the City Council of Birmingham, find three examples each of a) prepositional verbs, b) noun plus prepositional phrase.

   The City Council is committed to a policy of equal opportunities – examining the key issues and strengthening the links between the Council and minority ethnic and disadvantaged groups within the City.
   In 1984 the Race Relations and Equal Opportunities Committee was set up to work for the elimination of discrimination on the grounds of race, ethnic origin or disability and to promote equality of opportunity for minority ethnic and disabled people.
   The Race Relations and Equal Opportunities Unit has been set up to support the work of the Committee and over the past 2 years we have looked at key issues in the areas of employment and service provision. We are now seeking to strengthen our links with the community and relevant statutory and voluntary bodies concerned with improving race relations and promoting equal opportunities by making the following new appointments to the Unit: (…).

2. Put in the (eleven different) prepositions which have been deleted from the following newspaper article:
   a) The project was set … … the London borough … Newham … 1984.
   b) … it is the belief that … situations … conflict an impartial third person is needed who is trusted … both sides.
   c) The service started … response … disputes … the community.
   d) Most … the problems dealt … are described … "general nuisance" and most are … people … different cultural and ethnic backgrounds.
   e) Members gain experience … workshops and working … experienced mediators.
   f) In most conflicts the source is often deeper than the specific problem complained … .
   g) This approach … tensions can be seen to be treating the symptoms rather than the causes.
   h) The Home Office, too, is now looking … alternative ways … dealing … domestic disputes concerning the criminal justice system.
   i) Such projects may well lead the way … more human solutions … the rising tensions … our inner cities.
   (Adapted from *The Guardian*, October 10, 1986.)

3. Translate the second paragraph of the text *Relations with the police – a personal view*, from "Anyway, the next morning…" to "… where are we going" (p.53).

Nuclear power and an old forest — Unit 32

A
Nuclear power and the risks 👁

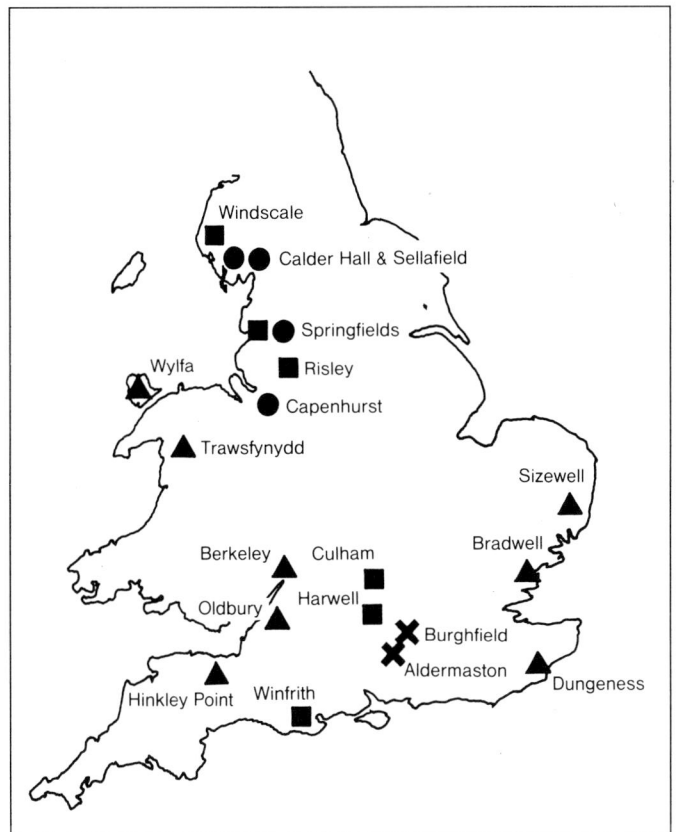

Nuclear installations in England and Wales

▲ nuclear power station

● nuclear military site

■
✗ } other nuclear establishments

(From: *New Scientist*, February 26, 1987, p. 22.)

Nuclear power stations produce only about 15 per cent of the electricity consumed in the United Kingdom. Until recently, this kind of energy had been growing because it seemed safer and cleaner than other sources like coal. The risks involved in **nuclear energy** were not really taken seriously. More and more nuclear power stations were built, usually along rivers and the coast where water could be used for cooling. People in all parts of the U.K. became used to living close to such power stations and other nuclear installations.

Environmentalists, too, were less active in the U.K. than elsewhere, e.g. in the USA or in West Germany. At least there seemed to be less public attention to environmental problems like nuclear radiation. In fact, even today the opposition to nuclear arms seems to be stronger than the resistance to nuclear power stations. However, the Windscale Nuclear Plant near **Sellafield** has been in the international news because radioactive waste from abroad is being collected there and radioactive leaks have been reported.

But two accidents outside the U.K. have made many people aware of the risks caused by the great number of nuclear installations along the coast (cf. map above). Since **Harrisburg** (USA) and **Chernobyl** (USSR) people have been worried not only about the possibility of a big blow-up, but also about the less spectacular leak of radioactivity from such installations. These emissions threaten to pollute the air and the water, and this way plants, animals and human-beings as well. Recent investigations by medical and scientific experts have brought to light mysterious rises in cancer in the neighbourhood of such nuclear plants (cf text on p.58). Officials are not yet prepared to blame such **health risks** on nuclear energy, and no mass movement exists to stop its production. But public opinion in the U.K. and elsewhere may change quickly if new accidents happen or the dangers become too serious to live with. At present, only small groups of people want to get rid of nuclear energy because the risks seem beyond control and because future generations would have to live with **dangerous waste** for a long time. If no technical safety can be reached for the operation of nuclear power plants, the nuclear dreams of the fifties may turn into a headache, not only for people in the United Kingdom.

Words

nuclear /'nju:klɪə/ – concerning atomic energy or the atom bomb; *site* – place; *establishment* – cf. installation; *installation* – apparatus in a fixed state (Einrichtung); *environmentalist* – person who tries to prevent the environment (Umwelt) from being spoilt; *radiation* – radioactivity (Strahlung); *plant* (n) – (here:) factory; *waste* (n) – used, damaged, unwanted matter (Abfall); *emission* – something which is being sent out; *investigation* – examination; *cancer* – diseased growth of cells, often causing death (Krebs); *blame on* – consider someone or something responsible for something.

Questions

1. Why have nuclear power stations been built in recent years, and why mostly along rivers and the coast?
2. Why are people getting worried about the nuclear production of electric power?

Contents of the documentary film, part A

The film takes Linda to Wales. Along the mouth of the River Severn no less than three nuclear power stations have been built (cf. map). After some small talk about Linda's trip, the weather, and the tide in the river estuary, Brian Price, who works in the harbour, gets down to the cause of his fears. He is very afraid of Berkeley Power Station which is right across the river.
Mr Price clearly opposes nuclear power especially since the accident at Chernobyl:

> "God forbid if you have the same accident over there as they did in Chernobyl, what chance have we got? What chance have the people of the forest got? This isn't any different except I feel that if the nuclear waste did get out of the station, it's into the estuary – it can travel 30 miles down, 30 miles back within hours. Once again, the Chernobyl incident has caused people now to start thinking, 'What have we got on our doorstep? Is it an asset?'
> I say, 'No'."

Even at present, with no accident and under normal circumstances radioactivity seems to get into the air and the water. This point seems to worry him very much since the tidal water could quickly spread any pollution within a wide radius. The alternative that he suggests would be tidal power used to produce electric energy. At present, the government does not seem to take the risks of nuclear power seriously:

> "The amount of survey work being done in the estuary to … not to combat it, because nobody can combat an incident, if it happens … but to measure the amount of radiation which is being leaked out over there, either into the atmosphere or into the water. It's being checked by the Ministry and the water authorities. But I still feel not enough is being done."

Linda's second talk about nuclear radiation is concerned with the recent discovery of leukaemia in the neighbourhood. As a member of the Severnside Campaign Against Radiation, aptly abbreviated SCAR, Sue Haverly takes careful notice of any damage to people's health that might be related to nuclear radiation from the energy plants. And the cases of childhood cancer reported so far are certainly alarming. According to Sue, the government must do more to watch over people's health and protect them. The best way would be to do without nuclear power as soon as possible. Here is what Sue and her group have stated as their aims:

> "Well, initially our aim was that there must be a public inquiry into the incidence of these childhood cancers and the possibility of a link between those and the emissions from the power stations.
> We feel there also must be much more extensive monitoring in the area of radiation levels. We also feel that the monitoring of our health is not sufficiently done, considering there is a hazard in this area, i.e. the nuclear power stations.
> People's health must be monitored much more carefully so people can actually know what's happening to them and if there is a danger from these installations, which we are told are perfectly safe."

Linda and Sue agree about this slogan of the environmentalist movement:

> "We do not inherit the earth from our ancestors; we borrow it from our children."

Words

estuary /ˈestjʊərɪ/ – mouth of a river into which the sea enters at high tide; *asset* – valuable or useful quality; *tidal* – related to the rise and fall of the seas; *leukaemia* /ljuːˈkiːmɪə/ – disease in which the blood contains too many white cells; *damage* (n) – harm; *monitor* (v) – take careful note of information, observe closely; *inherit* – receive from parents or ancestors after death; *ancestor* – person from whom one's father or mother is descended (Vorfahre).

Questions

3. What is it that makes Mr Price so afraid of nuclear power stations?
4. What are some of the aims of the Severnside Campaign Against Radiation (SCAR)?

*How dangerous is nuclear radiation?

After the accident at Chernobyl, large parts of Eastern and central Europe were polluted by radioactive fallout. Vegetables and milk had to be destroyed because they could have done harm to people's health. Ever since, many people have been worried about how dangerous nuclear radiation really is.

Here is what the environmentalist group SCAR has written in one of their pamphlets concerning the power stations in their neighbourhood:

> Two Magnox nuclear power stations, Berkeley and Oldbury, are situated on the River Severn estuary opposite the town of Lydney. The Central Electricity Generating Board, who operate the nuclear stations, have given assurances that there have been no leaks of radioactivity. However, over a five year period there have been 6 cases of childhood cancers all involving children under 8 years old and occurring within four miles of the power stations. Three of these cancers have occurred in a village of 1000 people – Netherend.

More recently, disturbing news has come from other nuclear sites in England and Wales as well. More cases of cancer than usual were found especially among children living close to nuclear installations. Note how careful both researchers and reporters are about drawing conclusions from the findings described in this article:

> The latest data on the incidence of childhood cancers around the military plants in Berkshire and Oxfordshire augment a preliminary analysis published last year (*New Scientist*, 30 January 1986, p. 24). Included for the first time are the cases of children contracting leukaemia who were referred outside the relevant health authority for diagnosis and treatment.
>
> This more complete analysis – which also includes details on cancer rates from the neighbouring health authority and around the Harwell research establishment – revealed a significant increase in cases in children under 14 years old. Most cases were in children aged less than four years. The incidence was more than double the expected rate based on the average for England and Wales (29 cases observed, 14.4 expected). The authors of the report, from the London School of Hygiene and Tropical Medicine, Basingstoke District Hospital and the Royal Berkshire Hospital, emphasise that although the excess cases are significant statistically, the actual risk of developing leukaemia to children living within 10 kilometres of the plants is "not great". The raised incidence represents one extra case per year of leukaemia among the 60 000 children surveyed.
>
> (...)
>
> The researchers concluded that there was no indication of an abnormal pattern of leukaemia around the board's nuclear power stations though they do highlight "abnormalities" in the incidence and mortality rate of liver cancers in persons aged between 25 and 74 living near four stations: Bradwell, Wylfa, Hinkley and Dungeness.
>
> (From: *New Scientist*, March 12, 1987, p. 17.)

Words

fallout – air polluted by radiation; *assurance* – certainty; *augment* /ɔːgˈment/ (v) – make greater; *preliminary* – not final; *contract* /kənˈtrækt/ (v) – get (a disease); *refer* – (here:) send to; *rate* (n) – number per unit; *excess* /ɪkˈses/ (n) – too many; *develop* – (here:) get (a disease); *indication* – sign; *highlight* (v) – point out, show.

Questions

5. What kinds of nuclear installations are mentioned in the article?
6. In two sentences summarize the main results of the research findings.

B

A strange border and an old forest

A stream winds its way through the unspoilt forest

The boundaries separating England from Scotland and Wales are not borders in a modern sense. In fact, as a tourist you will not notice much as you cross over into either Scotland or Wales. Along with Northern Ireland, England, Scotland and Wales form the political and economic unit of the United Kingdom.

Historically, however, these divisions have been important. And even today many cultural and linguistic differences remain, most visible perhaps in the bilingual street signs of Welsh towns and in the separate football teams for England, Wales, and Scotland. Other parts of our film series are concerned with such cultural borders.

59

The historical and geographical border between England and Wales runs through a characteristic area called the Border Country. Even today this land looks like some lost or forgotten country with unspoilt countryside and an impressive old royal forest, the Forest of Dean. In this no-man's-land not even the borderline itself is clearly established.

Question
7. What is the difference between "Great Britain" and the "United Kingdom"?

Contents of the documentary film, part B

In this part of our series, Linda is travelling through the **Border Country** and meets John Morgan there. He is a Welsh writer and a well-known radio broadcaster, but also a native of this strange region between England and Wales. When they are crossing the **River Wye**, this is what Linda learns about this borderline:

> "You see the trouble with the river here, the Wye, is that everyone assumes it's the border.
> And in a way it ought to be, because it's a beautiful border to have, isn't it?
> However, it's not true, I am afraid, because you could think you're going from England to Wales, and you could well be going from England to England.
> Or in some cases you could be going from Wales to Wales. I mean, a little further down here, for example, on each side of the river is Wales. And here, who knows? I mean this could be England, could be Wales. I don't know. I mean people just don't know.
> (…)
> But I certainly know, down there it's Wales on both sides. And up there, it could be England on both sides. But I suppose there are …, some people would be happier if it were clearcut."

John also explains to Linda that in the **Forest of Dean**, marked off by two rivers, some old and strange privileges have survived for the inhabitants and their sheep.

At the end of this film, **Jake Thackray** makes his appearance in a pub. He is the author of the signature tune *Crossing Borders*. But in this presentation he is more humorous and the song he has himself written and sings is more difficult to understand (cf. the text of the song).

Question
8. What makes the Border Country so unusual?

*Jake Thackray's song

There once was an old captain
Who wished nothing more
Than to live again his voyages
And walk by the seashore.

A simple man and a good man,
But the bane of his life
Was his ill-tempered, bad-hearted
Bitch of a wife.

Though the jolly captain
Was plagued by her bile,
He smoked his long pipe
And he smiled upon her tenderly.

He didn't like her much,
But he loved her
Despite her rough tone.
The wry-faced old no-good
Had been his pretty darling once.

She fell down her staircase;
She fractured her neck.
She lay upon the linoleum
In a black apoplexy.

Her baleful eyes bulged
With unspeakable abuse.
It seemed that her spleen
had been overproducing.

So the jolly captain
Carried her to bed.
"Close your poor eyes",
He said,
"Sleep a little peaceably."

He brought her fresh butter
And cool watercress,
Violet and peppermint
To soothe her heart's bitterness.

From her deathbed she said,
"If you marry when I die,
I'll crawl from my coffin
To haunt you vexatiously."

With a howl and a scowl,
With a shudder and a shake,
She spat out her peppermint
And went to vex her Maker.

Although, by God, so sad when she died.
He closed her wild eyes.
And he cried a bit on the Friday,
But saw no good reason for wasting away,
So he married an apple-cheeked girl
On the Saturday.

Alas, jolly captain,
You've married too soon.
She'll come to torment you
From underneath her tombstone.

She'll scratch and she'll scrape
Her way up from the grave,
Hacking her way back again
With furious fingernails.

"No", said the jolly captain,
"She'll stay in her place.
She can hack, she can claw,
Till she's black in the face.

No, she won't come to haunt me
And taunt me, I know,
'cause I buried her face downward
She's a long way to go."

Words

bane – cause of bad things; *bitch* – female dog, bad woman; *bile* – bad temper; *fracture* (v) – break; *apoplexy* – stroke; *baleful* – evil; *abuse* /əˈbjuːs/ (n) – bad language, curses; *watercress* – hot-tasting plant used for salads; *haunt* (v) – visit regularly (especially of spirits); *vexatious* /vekˈseɪʃəs/ – displeasing, troublesome; *torment* /tɔːˈment/ (v) – cause to suffer great pain; *tombstone* – gravestone; *scratch, scrape* (v) – rub and tear; *hack* (v) – cut up; *taunt* (v) – try to make angry.

Questions

9. Read the song aloud and find out why it does *not* quite sound like a poem.
10. What makes the song humorous (watch the audience react), and what do you think of this kind of humour?

C
Focus on language: Conditional clauses

Conditional clauses, or "if-then" conditions are very useful when we think about conditions and their consequences. Conditional if-clauses should therefore not be confused with temporal when-clauses:

    (1) **If** you marry **when** I die, I'll crawl from my coffin.

"When I die" refers to a point in time even though it is not known. But "if you marry" describes a situation which may or may not come true. If it comes true, the captain's wife promises to crawl from her coffin.

– In conditional clauses the dependent if-clause never goes with the conditional "would/should". The "would/should" conditional is reserved for the main (then-)clause:

    (2) Some people *would* be happier **if** it (the border) *were* clearcut.
    (3) **If** your *were* to come in the winter, the river *would* be quite turbulent.

– The if-clauses express how likely or possible the condition is considered to be. Sentence (2) gives an almost impossible situation because it is unrealistic to expect a clearcut border along a river. Sentence (3) is more likely, but Linda will probably not come back in the winter. Unreal conditions always ask for the Past Tense in the if-clause.

If-clauses can also describe neutral if-then conditions. These may refer to the future:

    (4) **If** you *come* back in three hours' time, you *will see* a volume of water …

Or they express something which is generally true (at least in the mind of the speaker):

    (5) Nobody *can combat* an accident **if** it *happens*.

Exercises

1. Not all of the following sentences contain conditional clauses. Insert "if" and "when" at the right places and put in the right verb form:
   a) ... a tidal power plant (build) in the Severn River estuary, it (can produce) up to ten times more energy than a nuclear power station.
   b) ... you (want to see) modern tidal power plants, you (have to travel) to either France or the Soviet Union.
   c) ... a dam (build) across the river to form a pond, it (fill) with water as the tide comes in.
   d) ... the pond water (return) to the ocean at ebb tide, it (channel) through a turbine and (generate) power.
   e) ... the turbines (design) well, a tidal power plant (have) a long and reliable life.
   f) ... the pond (be) large enough, it (can subdivide) into high and low levels.
   g) ... the tidal range (be) small, large and costly turbines (require).
   h) ... a tidal dam (build), it (bring) permanent changes to the fish and bird population.
   i) ... you (compare) the costs, a tidal power plant (can build) at the price of a nuclear power station.
   j) ... the government (decide to stop) wave-power research, most British research in this area (end).

   (Adapted from: *Technology Review*, July 1983, pp. 51-69.)

2. Translate into German what Sue Haverly has stated as the aims of her group, the Severnside Campaign Against Radiation. Cf. contents of part A, from: "Well, initially ..." to "... perfectly safe" (p.57).

3. Write a comment of approximately 120 words on this environmentalist slogan:

   "We do not inherit the earth from our ancestors; we borrow it from our children."

Wales and the Welsh   Unit 33

A

A Centre for Alternative Technology

Linda had crossed the border between England and Wales a number of times when she went to Lydney and to the Forest of Dean, situated between the Rivers Severn and Wye (see unit 32). Today we will follow her right into Wales. In Machynlleth, on the southern edge of the Snowdonia National Park, there is a Centre for Alternative Technology, which Linda wanted to visit in order to find out what people in the U.K. do to fight against pollution and to save energy.
Before we join Linda at the Centre, let us first take a **general look at Wales.**

"For a long time Wales was a country on its own, and different parts of it were ruled by kings and princes. Seven hundred years ago, however, it was gradually conquered and brought under the control of the rulers of England. More than 450 years ago, in the reign of Henry VIII, Wales and England were formally joined together...
Wales is a small country, of 8,000 square miles, about half the size of Switzerland. It has almost 2,800,000 people, about the same population as New Zealand or Israel. Indeed, it has far more sheep than people, about six million of them. Wherever you go in Wales you will see the sheep, woolly specks high up in the mountains and down in the green valleys, reminding you that much of rural Wales is made up of fairly small hill farms..."

(From: Trevor Fishlock, *Discovering Britain. Wales.* London and Boston 1979.)

"The southern part of Wales is different. A century ago it was the most intensively mined area of the world. People from northern Wales, England and Ireland, and even from Italy, Greece and Spain, came to work in the coal mines. At that time, and well into the 20th century, coal was much in demand. Cardiff, once a small town, became the 'coal capital' of the world. Even today you can tell the former industrial importance of South Wales by the rows after rows of terraced miners' houses, on steep hillsides, in the shadow of great heaps of coal waste."

(Adapted from: Trevor Fishlock, *Discovering...*)

Words
pollution /pəˈluːʃən/, from *pollute* – make air, water or soil dangerously impure (dirty) and unfit for use; *gradually* – slowly, step by step; *conquer* – take (land) by force; *terraced houses* – houses joined together in long rows.

Questions
1. What is the situation like in South Wales today? What do you think? (Remember what the miner from Wales told Linda when she met him at Betteshanger Colliery in Kent – unit 27 B! Think of the coal-mining industry in your own country, too!)
2. What would you expect to see and to learn in a centre for alternative technology?

Contents of the documentary film, part A

33

First, you will see some of the Welsh countryside as Linda drives through the Snowdonia National Park down to Machynlleth. Unfortunately, it was a rainy day. (You get a lot of rain in Wales, even in the summer, brought in from the sea by westerly winds.) But the pictures will still give you a rough idea of the beauty of the country.

Then you will follow Linda through the Centre for Alternative Technology. It is located in an old quarry near Machynlleth. Linda tries out some of the models they have there to show alternative ways of producing electricity – e.g. water wheels and windmills. In the **conservation house** she is joined by Tim Brown, the Press and Public Relations Officer of the Centre. He explains to Linda that the conservation house is very well insulated, with thick walls and four layers of glass in the windows. "A house like this will use maybe a tenth of the energy that a normal house will use", he says. – In the kitchen there are a number of energy-saving devices, e.g. insulated ovens and low-energy cookers.

Tim goes on to show Linda in what ways energy can be gained or saved. Here are some of his explanations:

"We get most of our energy from **renewable energy sources.** The first one is solar power. We have solar panels here, and they provide us with some hot water, especially during the summer, and with electricity. We also have quite a range of wind turbines, windmills, which produce electricity... for the lights and also for quite a lot of hot water. And we have a reservoir in our hills which is full of water, and that drives two water turbines. They produce about four kilowatts of electricity for the site (= the Centre). And that's really the most dependable source of energy in Wales, because it's always raining. So the reservoir is always full..."

The next thing Linda has a good look at is the **organic garden.** Here visitors are shown how to grow fruit and vegetables in a natural way, without using fertilizers. Again Tim Brown explains:

"A lot of people these days are worried about the effects of pesticides and fertilizers in agriculture. There's a big movement now in Britain for what's called organic food, organic growing. And this is a system of growing which is based on the natural cycle of fertility. And that's what we practise here, organic farming."

At the end of their tour Linda and Tim sit down in the restaurant where wholefood meals are served. Linda wants to know from Tim whether he thinks that the models she has seen at the Centre could be used **on a large scale basis.**

Tim:	They work fine for us. And there's no reason why they shouldn't work round the rest of the country.
Linda:	What would you do with a big city like Birmingham?
Tim:	Well, Birmingham is on the national electricity grid, and, if we had enough windmills around the country, that would supply electricity into the grid, and Birmingham would get the electricity that way.
	You won't get all your electricity from wind power all the time, but it would make a big contribution over the year.
	We're not saying everyone should have a windmill on their roof.
Linda:	Is the public interest growing though?
Tim:	Sure. We get a lot of people around every year. Many people are interested, especially because people are now worried about nuclear power, and they want to know what the alternatives are.
Linda:	Well, what about the Third World, do you get any visitors from there?
Tim:	Yeah, we do. A lot of the technologies which we have here are appropriate for developing countries as well as Britain.
Linda:	And do people actually go to their countries to help them? Or do you have a programme here?
Tim:	Yeah, we run training courses for people who are going out to developing countries to help with development projects.

Words

quarry (n)/ 'kwɒrɪ/ – place from which stone or sand is dug out; *insulate* – cover (something) so as to prevent the passing of electricity, heat, sound, etc.; *device* /dɪ'vaɪs/ – an instrument, esp. one that is cleverly thought out; *source* /sɔːs/ – a place from which something comes, e.g. the place where a river starts; *renewable source* – a source which can be used again and again; *panel* /'pænl/ – a board on which instruments are fastened; *solar panel* – a board to collect energy from the sun, e.g. by using solar cells; *dependable* – reliable, to be trusted; *fertilizer* /ˈfɜːtɪlaɪzə/ – a chemical or natural substance that is put on the land to make plants grow better; *pests* – small animals or insects that harm or destroy plants; *on a large scale basis* – in a big way; *electricity grid* – the network of wires connecting the power stations; *supply* (v) /səˈplaɪ/ – give things to a person for use; *contribute* /kənˈtrɪbjuːt/ – join with others in giving money or help.

Questions

3. At the Centre for Alternative Technology Linda was shown a number of ways to gain or save energy. Which ones do you remember? Write them down in two groups: (a) ways or methods to save energy; (b) methods to gain energy from renewable sources.
4. If the methods used at the Centre were put to use on a large scale basis, how would that effect the environment, that is the natural conditions, such as air, water, and land, in which we live? Will the use of alternative technologies only have positive effects, or can you think of any negative effects, too?
5. In the organic garden the people of the Centre do not use chemicals. What do they use instead to help their fruit and vegetables grow? Try to give three examples!

*Comments on the Centre from visitors, newspapers and magazines

If you would like to know what people think of the Centre for Alternative Technology, read the following comments which the people of the Centre have themselves collected in a brochure entitled *Ten Years at the Quarry. A Short History of the Centre for Alternative Technology* (Machynlleth, 1985):

> "I'm surprised the Government funds them." – "They must make a fortune with all those visitors!" – "Communists, that's what they are – and hippies!" – "Well, we've got a lot of solar power in Australia, but having come here I think I want to buy a wind turbine!" – "This is certainly the best holiday I have ever had!" (Visitors)

> "The exhibition is attracting 500 visitors a day ... Both Prince Philip and the Duke of Kent have chosen to make private visits and more than 90 companies have made contributions..." (*The Guardian*, 1975)

> "IT'S THE GOOD LIFE! Roderick James quit an architect's office. Jeremy Light chucked biological research. Jane Bryant took a break from architectural studies. Now they are at an old slate mine (quarry) in West Wales aiming to prove that urban man can create much of his own energy and partly feed himself." (*The Sun*, 1977)

The latter article refers to the fact that many of the people who work at the Centre have given up "normal" jobs – at least for a couple of years – in order to test alternative technologies and inform the public.

"At the outset one should say that this is not a haven for worn-out sixties' ideas or a home for tired old hippies. The approach to that problem which will not go away – how to husband the world's resources – is both scientific and pragmatic. The Centre lives in the real world and pays its bills..." (*Esso Magazine*, 1984)

Words

fund (v) – provide (give) money for an activity, organization, etc.; *quit* – finish with, go away from; *chuck* – give up (slang word); *urban man* – man living in a city; *outset* – beginning, start; *haven* – a place of safety; *worn-out* – completely finished by long use, like old shoes; *husband* (v) – use carefully, make the best use of something.

B
Croeso i Gymru – Welcome to Wales

Wales – a bilingual country

The major part of the British population are of Germanic origin; they belong to the language family that includes English, Swedish, Dutch, German, etc. The Welsh are different. They are Celts, like the Scots and the Irish. About 3,000 years ago the Celts started to spread all over Europe. Some 1,000 years later other peoples began to invade the western parts of Europe and the British Isles: Romans first; later Saxons, Vikings, Normans. Some of the Celts mixed with the newcomers, but most of them retreated to remote areas along the west coast, to the Scottish Highlands and across the Irish Sea.

To the Saxons who had settled in England, the Celts of Wales seemed very "different". This was not only because of their life-style but also because of their language. And it was the Saxons who named their neighbours in the west **Wealas** (foreigners). This old Saxon word was gradually changed to **Wales** and **Welsh**. In their own language, the Welsh call their country **Cymru** (Land of Brothers), and on the signs at the Welsh borders it says **Croeso i Gymru**, as you will have noticed in unit 32. In the 19th century the English tried hard to spread their own language in Wales. Welsh was no longer taught at schools, and children who spoke Welsh were punished. So the number of Welsh speaking people went down from more than 50% of the Welsh population in 1891 to just over 20% in 1971.

Now Welsh is being brought back to the schools, and all traffic and road signs are in English and Welsh, with Welsh in the first place, as you will see in the second part of the documentary film. Indeed, today Welsh is spoken by more people than any other Celtic language:

- **Welsh** – about 600,000 speakers
- **Breton** – about 500,000 speakers in Brittany in north-west France
- **Gaelic** – about 80,000 speakers, mainly in the Highlands and the western islands of Scotland
- **Irish** – about 70,000 speakers, mainly in western Ireland
- **Cornish** (formerly spoken in Cornwall) and **Manx** (Isle of Man) have died out.

(Adapted from: Trevor Fishlock, *Discovering...*)

Words

Celts /kelts/ – the original inhabitants of Europe and the British Isles; *retreat* – move back, especially when forced to do so; *remote* – far away, quiet and lonely; *Cymru* – Don't be surprised that "Cymru" suddenly becomes "Gymru" in "Croeso i Gymru". In Celtic languages the initial consonant changes under certain grammatical circumstances. In our case, the preposition "i" requires that initial "C" changes to a "G".

Contents of the documentary film, part B

In Dolgellau, another small and beautiful town on the west coast of Wales, Linda sees that all traffic, road and shop signs are in Welsh. In her hotel she asks the manager to find her somebody who speaks Welsh and will tell her about the role which the Welsh language plays in everyday life. The manager introduces her to Olwyn Lloyd Evans, a young lady who works at a local bank. Here is some of their conversation:

Olwyn: The Welsh language is the first language spoken here, and you will come across many signs. Have you any examples?
Linda: Yes, I've written this down in my notebook here. What's this, for example?
Olwyn: Oh, that is Betws-y-Coed and Tywyn and Porthmadog, which are all names of local towns.
Linda: Oh, so they're names.
Olwyn: Mmh.
Linda: Now, what about this sign?
Olwyn: That's Llwybr Cyhoeddus...

Linda:	Mmh?
Olwyn:	...which actually means 'public footpath'.
Linda:	Footpath!?
Olwyn:	Mmh, you'll see many signs like them... Welsh is the first language as I say and it is even spoken in the local schools and even in the bank where I work...
Linda:	And, when you went to school, did you learn Welsh or English?
Olwyn:	Oh, both languages. But Welsh, mainly Welsh, because that's the first language, and they do encourage it.
Linda:	They do!?
Olwyn:	Mmh.
Linda:	So this probably isn't Croeso i dref Dolgellau.
Olwyn:	That's Croeso i dref Dolgellau.
Linda:	Don't get it! That's the name of the town here?
Olwyn:	Yes, it actually means 'Welcome to Dolgellau'.
Linda:	Mmh.
Olwyn:	And if you actually split the name to two, 'dol', which gives you meadow, and 'gellau', hazeltrees.
Linda:	Oh, that's interesting. So there must be a lot of meadows with hazeltrees around here.
Olwyn:	Yeah, indeed. Yes.
Manager:	Coffee, ladies.
Linda:	How do you say 'thank you' in Welsh? (Olwyn whispers 'diolch'. Linda says it loud to the manager.)
Manager:	Sorry, I only speak English.

At the end of the film there are more pictures of the beautiful Welsh countryside. Along with them there is a choir singing a traditional song – in Welsh, of course!

Questions
6. Do you think Welsh and other minority languages should be kept alive? (Try to list the advantages and disadvantages!)
7. Why did the English try to suppress the Welsh language? Do you have any idea?
8. Do you know of other countries in which two or more languages are spoken?

*Fighting for the Welsh language

"Recently there have been major developments in the use of the Welsh language in primary school education so that Welsh is now used as a first language or taught as a second language in more than 75 per cent of the primary schools in Wales. As children are able to learn the language when they are young, this may help to prevent Welsh declining further.
There has been a growth of evening classes in Welsh .... For many jobs in Wales you now have to know Welsh. In 1962 the Welsh Language Society was formed. This society has made protests about the way they think the Welsh language is ignored. They want a television channel completely for

Welsh. At present there are just a few Welsh programmes on an English television channel. Because of this the society has attempted to interfere with television transmitters and to stop broadcasts. They have also interrupted courts of law where Welsh was not being used."

(From: John R. Love, *Wales*. London 1981, pp.24/25.)

Words
decline (v) – go down, move from a better to a worse position; *ignore* – take no notice of something; *attempt* (v) – try; *interfere* /ɪntəˈfɪə/ – get in the way of somebody else, block an action; *interrupt* /ɪntəˈrʌpt/ – break the flow of something, e.g. a speech.

C
Focus on language: Word-formation

It is quite useful to know a few things about how words are formed, because knowledge about word-formation helps us to understand or, at least, guess the meaning of words we have not yet come across.

You can form a new word by placing a **prefix** at the beginning or a **suffix** at the end of a word or base. Here is an example:

new + prefix **re-** (meaning "again") → **renew** – make something as good as new again, give new life to something.

Of course you will have noticed that by this word-formation we have not only given the original word a slightly different meaning, but we have also turned it from an adjective into a verb.

We can continue the process by adding different endings to our "new" word:

(1) **renew** (verb) + suffix **-al** → **renewal** (noun) – the act of renewing.
(2) **renew** (verb) + suffix **-able** → **renewable** – an adjective we have come across in the phrase "renewable sources of energy".

Exercises
1. Change the following nouns into adjectives by using the appropriate suffix!
   centre, nature, nation, practice, physics, mathematics, geography, logic

2. Try to form at least three new words each by adding prefixes and/or suffixes to the following words:
   organ /ˈɔːgən/ (noun) – a part of an animal or plant that has a special purpose
   develop /dɪˈveləp/ (verb) – cause to grow, bring out the possibilities of something, e.g. an industry or a country
   nation (noun) – a large group of people living in one area and usually having an independent government

3. In many cases you can turn a verb into different nouns by using different suffixes. Example:
   found → (a) *founder* – a person who starts to build up a castle, an organization, etc.
   → (b) *foundation* – the act or result of founding
   Try to do the same with the verbs *act, produce, invent, inspect, insulate.*

4. Scientists and technicians use a lot of *technical terms*. For many people these are "hard words"; they are difficult to understand because they are often of foreign origin, mostly Latin or Greek. However, they are being used internationally. So, if you know quite a bit about e.g. alternative technology or organic gardening because you have read German books about these subjects, you will find English books about the same subjects easy to read since the "hard words" are (almost) the same in both languages. Only the pronunciation is often different.

   Go back to the contents of part A (pp. 65–66). Read again what Tim Brown told Linda about alternative energy and organic gardening. Underline the technical terms he used. Which ones are almost the same in German?

5. Translate Tim Brown's explanation in the contents of part A, from "We get most of our energy..." to "So the reservoir is always full" (pp. 65–66).

Two Northern Irish towns — Unit 34

A
What's in a name?

A divided town

This unit is concerned with two towns in Northern Ireland. Incidentally, you will often hear Northern Ireland referred to as **Ulster**. This is merely the ancient name for this northern section of the island.

The first town we visit is **Londonderry**, Northern Ireland's second largest town. It is beautifully situated on the banks of the River Foyle and has much of interest to offer the visitor. The town walls, for instance, are still perfectly intact, which makes Londonderry one of the few completely walled towns left in Europe. And yet most visitors to Northern Ireland or to the north-west of the Republic of Ireland bypass it, which is certainly their loss.

Another point of importance about the town is that its history gives a wonderful insight into what is behind the so-called **Troubles** in Northern Ireland, so it is worth our while to take a brief look at its past and not just at its present.

The first event of importance happened just after the death of Queen Elizabeth I in 1603. As she died childless, her cousin James, who was already king of Scotland, succeeded her and became king of England as well. Soon after, James decided to intensify the policy of "Plantation" in Northern Ireland. This had nothing to do with plants but was another word used at the time for colonization. Under this policy thousands of Englishmen and Scotsmen went to Ulster and settled there.

James thought the "Plantation" of Ulster would enable him to kill two birds with one stone. Firstly, it would be a great new source of income for him. Secondly, he hoped in this way to solve the problem of Northern Ireland once and for all: in the past Ulster had always caused trouble and had constantly rebelled against the English. King James and his advisors were staunch Protestants and they thought the real root of the problem was that the Irish population in Ulster was Catholic. In contrast, the Scottish and English settlers that now came there in their thousands were all Protestant and therefore loyal to their king. Through their influence, James hoped Ulster would eventually become as obedient and law-abiding as the rest of his kingdom.

Unfortunately, James's policy did not solve any problems in Northern Ireland; it merely made them bigger. Trouble was bound to come, for after all the newcomers to Ulster were not only of a different race and religion; they were also from a totally different civilization. Add to this that a lot of the land that the English and Scottish settlers were able to buy for a song had been taken from the original Irish population in the first place.

By the way, it was at this time that the confusion about the town's name arose: Is it Derry or Londonderry? Under James the City of London had been persuaded to finance the rebuilding of the town of Derry and to find the people to settle there. It was to mark this connection with the British capital that Derry was renamed Londonderry in 1613. And that explains why to this day the Protestants insist on calling the town Londonderry and the Catholics on using the name Derry. For the Catholics, of course, the new name was, and still is, a symbol of British injustice and domination.

The discontent among the Irish population came to a head in **1641.** In that year they rebelled against their Protestant overlords and it was not till twelve years later that the uprising was finally put down. Probably some 10,000 Protestants were killed during the uprising and certainly not the 150,000 to 200,000 that Ulster Protestants were talking about 40 years later. At any rate the Ulster Protestants have never forgotten and, of course, never forgiven the killings.

Just over 40 years later, indeed, the uprising was going to play an important role again. Then James II, a Catholic, was trying to get the British throne back from William III, a Protestant. James II's plan was very simple: land in Ireland, strengthen his troops with an Irish army from the Catholic South, quickly defeat the Ulster Protestants, land in Scotland, where he had more supporters, and then go south to take care of William. His plan seemed to be working well until **1689** when his Catholic troops stood outside the gates of Londonderry.

Inside the walls of Londonderry the inhabitants remembered what had happened in 1641 and so refused to surrender: they were not going to believe any promises made by Catholics! James II laid siege to the town, but, at the cost of great suffering, it held out until help came 105 days later. This was the famous **Siege of Londonderry**. Shortly afterwards William III defeated James II in battle. It goes without saying that, because of their victory, the Protestants of Londonderry, and indeed of the whole of Ulster, became even more fanatically determined to stay as closely connected as possible with the British and to have nothing to do with the Catholic South of the island. The divisions between the original Irish population and the English and Scottish community in Ulster went so deep after 1689 that they are still decisive for daily life in Northern Ireland today.

Words

What's in a name – the title is adapting a quotation from Shakespeare's *Romeo and Juliet*; *intact* – complete or whole; *Troubles* – the normal word for the political and social disorders in Northern Ireland, especially as connected with the bombings and killings; *childless* – without a child; *settle* – go and live in a place; *kill two birds with one stone* – get two good results from one action; *loyal* – faithful and true to one's country, etc.; *law-abiding* – obedient to the law, keeping the law; *be bound to* – be sure or certain to; *for a song* – very cheaply, for a very low price; *come to a head* – reach a crisis; *uprising* – rising against one's rulers, the government, etc.; *lay siege to* /siːdʒ/ (n) – surrounding a town or army, etc., constantly attacking and refusing to let any supplies get through.

Questions

1. Are the "Troubles" in Ulster merely a religious problem? What other elements are important in your eyes?
2. Do you think the British and Irish governments will ever be able to find a solution to the Ulster problem that will satisfy all parties?

Contents of the documentary film, part A

The film first gives us quite a few impressions of the town of Londonderry/Derry. Then we see Maureen Gallagher on her way to work at Radio Foyle. On the car radio, she was listening to a broadcast from the local fire station. A colleague of hers was just being strapped on to the safety hook on the top extension of a turntable ladder. The fireman assisting the reporter assured her that she was safe enough since all the equipment was tested every 3 months. When the ladder had been fully extended, they started rotating it, so that the reporter had a beautiful view of the city and of the River Foyle as far as the estuary. She could even see right into her office at Radio Foyle.

On arriving at Radio Foyle, Maureen Gallagher started work in one of the studios. After she had announced that she was handing over to another reporter who would give the listeners an update on the sports results, she turned round to Linda, who had been waiting in the studio as well for an opportunity to ask her some questions.

Linda: What kind of station is Radio Foyle?
Maureen: Well, we're very much a small community station. We're part of the BBC, but we operate very much for the listeners in the north-west. So that means we make programmes very much about issues that concern local people. We spend a lot of time out in the radio car getting to meet them, that kind of thing. On the way to work I was listening to a programme from the local fire station. So that's an example of the kind of thing we get involved in.

Linda then wanted to know what the conflict, the fact of being a divided city, meant for the station.

Maureen: Well, it doesn't mean anything in particular in one sense. Obviously, if there is a killing or a bombing or a shooting, we report it in our news. But we're much more concerned with getting on with everyday living. It's not something that we think about all the time.

Maureen also told her that there were Catholics and Protestants in the community, but that they didn't consciously try to make sure they had the same number of Protestants on each programme as Catholics. Their programmes reflected the people who were interested in the station, the inhabitants of Londonderry or, as most locals say, Derry.

Words

strap – fasten or secure with straps (= leather bands); *safety hook* – a curved piece of metal or plastic which the straps are put into to stop the person from falling; *update* – a report which brings the latest information; *sports results* – e.g. the final scores of football matches, which horse won a horse-race, who won a tennis match, etc.; *issue* (n) – important question or subject; *conflict* – battle or dispute (in this case which has caused Londonderry to become a divided city); *news* – regular update on recent events which is broadcast on radio or television.

Questions

3. What does Maureen Gallagher say they are mainly concerned about at Radio Foyle? What is the service they are trying to offer?
4. Can you see any similarities between Berlin and Londonderry/Derry?

*If Londonderry had surrendered…!

The Siege of Londonderry is one of the big "ifs" of history. What would have happened if Londonderry had surrendered to James II's army in 1689?

Well, in that case, James would have been able to go across to Scotland with his army to join his supporters there. Then he would have been able to march down through England to London, where William would have been waiting for him nervously. Nervously? Yes, because he was new on the throne and a foreigner as well (he was Dutch), so he could by no means be sure how loyal his new subjects would be to him. In other words, James might have had a good chance of winning. And this would have changed the whole course of English history. For example, James was a Catholic. It is probably going too far to say that his kingdom might have become Catholic again. But certainly Catholics would have had a bigger say in the country's destinies and later in the British Empire, and so on and so forth!

However, James's master plan was ruined by Londonderry's refusal to surrender. This meant that James could not take the war to England as quickly as he wanted to and that William was given valuable time to prepare better for the conflict with James. Instead of James coming to England, William crossed to Ireland, where he defeated James.

In this way, William firmly established British rule in Ulster and at the same time cemented the divisions there.

(An idea based on and adapted from a passage in the foreword of Patrick Macrory's book *The Siege of Derry,* Hodder and Stoughton. London 1980, pp. 11–12.)

Words

supporter – a person loyal to another person or an idea; *subject* – a person owing loyalty to a state or ruler; *and so on and so forth* – a phrase used at the end of a list of things to suggest that one could make the list still longer.

Question

5. If James II had won, the history of Britain, of Europe and even of the world would almost certainly have been changed in a number of points. Can you suggest any other effects his winning instead of William could have had?

B
The Unsinkable? ⚏

The docks: symbol of Belfast's former greatness

The second town we visit in Ulster is **Belfast, the first town and capital of Northern Ireland.** A town grew up here on the River Lagan for exactly the same reason that London grew up on the River Thames: Belfast was located at a river crossing and provided a strategically well-placed site for a sea port.

In addition to the Scottish and English immigrants at the beginning of the 17th century, a large number of French Huguenots arrived here at the end of the same century. They brought improved methods of weaving with them, which gave birth to a thriving linen industry in Belfast. Belfast also developed into an important port for the import of tobacco from America, so that in time Belfast also became famous for its tobacco industry and associated businesses like pipemaking.

On the one hand, coal was required from England and Scotland for the manufacture of linen; on the other, both the linen and tobacco industries needed ships to export their products. This meant that in the course of the 19th century another major industry grew up in Belfast, shipbuilding. The three largest ports in the United Kingdom at this time were London, Liverpool and Belfast.

In the meantime, unfortunately, the town has fallen on hard times and unemployment is now high. Perhaps it was not a good omen that the "Titanic" was built here. However, if the "Titanic" proved indeed not to be "unsinkable" as its builders claimed, Belfast maintains a vitality and vigour which immediately strikes the visitor, who soon understands why this city could hold the key to the future not just of Ulster but of the whole of Ireland.

Words
grow up – arise, come into being; *Huguenots* /ˈhjuːgənɔːts/ – a group of French Protestants in the 16th and 17th centuries; *weaving* – the art of making cloth by drawing threads under and over other threads; *thriving* – see unit 28, p.22; *linen* – a type of cloth made from the plant flax (= Flachs); *fall on hard times* – become poor.

Contents of the documentary film, part B

After passing through security, Linda joined Frances Kennedy and was extremely surprised that she was being picked up in a brand-new bus.
Frances first introduced her to Mr Werner Heubeck, the Managing Director of the local bus company. Mr Heubeck told Linda that a visitor from Germany was always welcome and then invited her on board the bus to see the sights of Belfast.

When they came to Queen's University, Frances told her she knew it well because she had done a post-grad year there, although she had spent more time in the Students' Union opposite, because that was where the bar was. She said there were about 3000 students at Queen's. The university had a big extramural department and there was a Queen's festival of folk music there every year, too. It was an important part of Belfast, Frances continued, and Belfast would be a lot poorer without it. Frances also told Linda that the most important thing about the university was that it was non-sectarian.

In downtown Belfast they saw that a lot of people were out shopping because it was a Saturday afternoon. Linda asked what the banner on City Hall meant which said "Belfast says No".

> Frances: It's a protest by the Loyalist community, the majority, the Protestants you can say. And they're more or less saying "No" to a coming together of the two parts of Ireland. This is..., it's really a protest banner I suppose you can say.

Later on their tour of the city, they saw one of the urban redevelopment areas. Formerly there had been a lot of flats and houses there without toilets and bathrooms. This was a very successful example of urban redevelopment. Although there had been many changes since Frances had been a wee girl there, they were basically the same people who still lived in the area, because somehow the people responsible had managed to move the people back into their own communities after the building work had been completed.
As a contrast, they then saw a bad example of urban redevelopment – or a real eyesore as Frances called it. The flats had been built in the sixties and from the very beginning the people had protested against having to live there. At the time of Linda's visit they were in the process of demolishing them

and were hoping to replace them with the same type of houses Linda and Frances had seen shortly before.

At the end of the tour, Linda asked Mr Heubeck what a German was doing in Belfast as Managing Director of the local bus company. He replied that he had been in Belfast for 21 years and had come over when the bus company had had some financial troubles. When Linda said Frances had told her that the last time he had driven one of his buses personally was because there had been a bomb in it, Mr Heubeck answered that, if you lived in Northern Ireland, you got used to all sorts of things, including dealing with bombs and other serious matters. He regarded Belfast as his home and thought he would be there for the rest of his days.

The last thing that Frances showed Linda in Belfast was Belfast Castle, which was being renovated because it had been petrol-bombed about a year before.

> Frances: You get a beautiful view from here.
> Linda: Look at the harbour.
> Yes, the view really is splendid.
> Frances: Great, isn't it?
> Linda: Sure is. What's it like for you coming back here after all those years? What is it that you miss?
> Frances: It's been a long time, but I just love coming back. I love it every time. But you know, when I really think about it, although Belfast isn't the greatest place on earth, I miss the people and the warmth.

Words

security – the area where you and your belongings are searched for weapons and bombs; *managing director* – the chief executive or head manager in an organization; *the sights* – the things worth seeing in a place, especially by tourists; *post-grad* – short for "post-graduate": a "post-grad year" is a year of studies done after taking the first university degree; *Students' Union* – building where students have a social life together; *extramural department* – a department offering day and evening courses for people who are not full-time students of the university; *non-sectarian* – open to students of all religions; *downtown* – American for city centre; *banner* – a long piece of cloth with a sign on it; *Loyalists* – the Protestants in Northern Ireland are politically known as "Loyalists" (loyal to the British throne) or "Unionists" (wanting to be united fully to Great Britain). The Catholics are normally known as "Republicans" (wanting to be united with the Republic of Ireland) or "Nationalists" (wanting the whole of Ireland to be one nation); *urban redevelopment* – for "urban" and "development" see unit 28, p.26); *Belfast Castle* – this was a mansion (= large private house) built in 1870 and given to the city of Belfast in 1934.

Questions

6. Urban redevelopment has been going on in Belfast since the sixties, but not everyone in Belfast is happy about the results. Can you suggest why people should be worried about what the redevelopment is doing to the town?
7. Linda read a banner on City Hall with the words "Belfast says No". Do you know what it is specifically they are saying "No" to?

*Is there a solution?

The following text is taken from a book by Kevin Boyle and Tom Hadden called *Ireland. A Positive Proposal* (a Penguin Special, London 1985, p.11). It has been highly praised as giving a realistic assessment of the situation in Ulster and what can be done to change it. These are their opening words:

"Ireland is Britain's oldest problem. Britain is Ireland's. Ever since Britain became directly involved in the government of Ireland in the twelfth century there has been intermittent strife and warfare. This has traditionally been portrayed as a conflict between the British imperial state – and those it settled in Ireland – and the native Irish population. The fact that the peoples of the two islands have been inextricably mingled for thousands of years has thus been obscured. The native population of Ireland is the cumulation of successive waves of settlers from Britain and Europe. The British people is an equally complex mixture in which there has always been a very substantial Irish contribution. But this has not prevented the development of opposing national identities. The British and the Anglo-Irish are – or were – rich, Protestant and a dominant force in European and world politics. The Irish are Catholic, relatively poor and committed to neutrality. During the latter part of the nineteenth century these divergent identities became increasingly marked . . . .

The Irish problem was partially resolved in 1921-2 by a treaty between Britain and the Irish Free State that granted effective independence to most of Ireland. . . within the Commonwealth.

The problem was only partially resolved because, then as now, a substantial majority of the people in the six north-east counties of Ireland wanted nothing to do with either home rule or an independent Ireland and had shown themselves to be ready and able to fight against them . . . ."

Words
intermittent – happening from time to time with pauses in between; *strife* – trouble between people; *warfare* – making war; the condition of being at war; *inextricably* – so tied together that cannot be separated; *mingle* – mix with.

Question
8. What is the rather surprising fact that the authors bring to our attention about the British and the Irish?

C
Focus on language: this, there, it

As you have seen, **this** is a very useful word when you're acting as a guide. You can use **this** to draw people's attention to something new, like when you introduce new people:

> **This** is Mr Heubeck.

Or when you point out new places of interest:

> **This** is Queen's University, the red-brick building on your right.

Another way of introducing a new subject of conversation or new information so far not mentioned is to use **there is** and **there are** (in other tenses as well of course):

> **There's** an extramural department at Queen's.
> How many students **are there** at Queen's?

With **there is** and **there are** you can also tell someone that something simply exists:

> Of course **there's** a God. (= Of course God exists.)
> The British people is an equally complex mixture, in which **there has** always **been** a very substantial Irish contribution. (= A substantial Irish contribution has always existed in the British people.)

It, on the other hand, refers back to something that has already been mentioned. **It** therefore helps you to avoid unnecessary repetition.

> The equipment's all tested. **It**'s tested every 3 months.
> We're right in the city centre. **It**'s very busy.

We also use **it** in cases where the subject of a sentence would otherwise be too long and clumsy. Compare, for example, the following pairs of sentences:

> To work and study at the same time is very difficult.
> **It** is very difficult to work and study at the same time.

> Telling me you can't understand this is no use.
> **It**'s no use telling me you can't understand this.

I think you will agree that the sentences beginning with **it** somehow "sound" better. Probably because they put the important information where it usually comes in an English sentence: at or very near the end of the sentence.

34

Exercises

1. Please use **it** to change the following sentences so that the important information comes at the end of the sentence.

   a) To work and study at the same time is very difficult.
   b) To do an Open University course thoroughly takes more than 19 hours a week.
   c) To talk over doing the course with your family is very important.
   d) That we could lose our jobs is at the back of all our minds.
   e) To give them as much fact to base their opinions on as possible is our job at *The Guardian*.

2. Please insert **it's** or **there is/are**, whichever you feel is correct.

   a) ... many people in Britain who are interested in what's called organic food.
   b) The ladder is going up higher. Now ... rotating.
   c) ... a lot to be said for learning English.
   d) I am glad to be back from my business trip. After all, ... no place like home, ...?
   e) ... not closing time yet, so ... time for another drink.

f) ... a time and a place for everything. And this isn't the time to fall asleep.
g) We must act immediately. ... no time to lose.
h) ... worth our while to take a brief look at Londonderry's past.
i) ... high time that something was done about this.
j) I'm afraid ... time to leave, otherwise we'll miss our train.

3. What words or expressions which have been explained in this chapter have the opposite meaning to the following?

a) lawless
b) out of date
c) opponent
d) sectarian
e) peace
f) undergraduate

Working towards reconciliation   Unit 35

A

Is the situation really hopeless? ൦ഠ

Children from both communities enjoying a holiday together.

A lot of people, both British and Irish, feel that there is no way out of the difficult situation in Northern Ireland. But is it really as hopeless as it looks at first sight?
There are a number of individuals and groups in Ulster who do not think so. They feel that there has been more than enough *talking* about the divisions in Northern Ireland, and that the time has now come to *do* something about healing them. These ordinary men and women have accordingly started to do what they can to bridge the great divide.
As we have not grown up in Ulster, it is extremely difficult for us to realize just how great that divide can be. The two sections of the community in Northern Ireland are separated in a whole variety of ways. Firstly, they normally live in different parts of town. So, for instance, there are districts in Londonderry and Belfast where only Catholics live, and others that are completely Protestant. Secondly, the children living in these separate parts of town often go to separate or denominational schools. That means they go either to schools that are completely Protestant or to schools that are totally Catholic. And the separation does not stop there: when the children go home from school, they return to their separate districts and play there, never having the chance to mix with children from the other side. It really is no exaggeration to say therefore that it is quite possible for a Protestant to grow up without ever meeting a Catholic, and vice versa. And this of course means that this separation from the other section of the community continues when they become adults, too, so that, as a rule, there are very few mixed marriages.

In recent years, a number of people have tried to break out of this vicious circle. They have attempted this in various ways, of which we will give three examples here.

Firstly, there is **Corrymeela**, which was founded by Ray Davey, a clergyman. Corrymeela, which means "hill of harmony" incidentally, is an open village, "open to all people of good will, who will meet each other, learn from each other and work together for the good of all". The basic idea is to provide a place on neutral ground where people from both sides can meet, can get to know each other, can discuss and pray together with no strings attached.

Others have taken a different approach: they say that the start should be made with the children, because after all it is they who will have the future of Northern Ireland in their hands. In recent years some integrated schools have been opened to take in children from both sides of the community. One of them is called **Hazelwood College** and is located in North Belfast. It was started by a group of Protestant and Catholic parents who got together to try and get a non-denominational school going. They were encouraged in their efforts by the fact that polls had shown that 2 out of 3 parents in Northern Ireland were in favour of not putting their children into separate schools.

For Hazelwood College, integration means more than just having Protestant and Catholic children under one roof. For the people at Hazelwood it also means making allowances for each other's traditions, learning from and about each other and drawing out what is best from both cultural backgrounds. The school's motto is "Facta non Verba", "Deeds not words" – we could translate it, certainly more freely but also more appositely perhaps, with the English saying "actions speak louder than words".

Another group also starts with the children. It is the example we take in the first documentary in this unit and is called **Holiday Projects West**. HPW provides holidays for younger children, most of whom would not get a holiday otherwise, and workcamps for 16 to 19 year olds, all of them from both sections of the community in the western area of Northern Ireland. HPW deliberately mixes the Protestant and the Catholic children in its groups.

HPW is undoubtedly exercising a very good influence in the Londonderry/Derry area. One of the people I met in a café there referred to the founder of HPW as "the beacon of light in this lunatic asylum".

Certainly, these are small beginnings, but there can be no doubt that they are a move in the right direction.

Words
heal – cause to become healthy or well again; *the great divide* – (here) the border between the two sections of the Ulster population; *denominational* – belonging to one religious denomination (= a particular religious body with its own separate beliefs); *vice versa* /ˈvaɪsɪˈvɜːsə/ – Latin for in the opposite way to what has just been stated (so it is just as possible for a Catholic to grow up without ever meeting a Protestant as well); *a mixed marriage* – a marriage between people of different races, religions or denominations; *vicious circle* – causes and effects which go round in circles (e.g. A causes B, B causes C, and C causes A again, and so it goes on and on; Teufelskreis); *clergyman* – a priest or minister of religion; *with no strings attached* – with no conditions, so that you don't commit yourself in any way; *integrated* – with a mixture of children from both sections of the Ulster population; non-denominational; *poll* or *opinion poll* – the result of questioning a representative

number of people to find out what the general opinion is; *make allowances for* – take facts into account that could change an opinion; *apposite* /'æpəʊzɪt/ – exactly suitable to the occasion, to the context, etc.; *lunatic asylum* – a hospital for people suffering from an illness of the mind. Nowadays, we avoid this expression and usually talk about a "mental hospital".

Questions
1. Do you think that the situation in Northern Ireland, based as it is on centuries of conflict, is hopeless? If not, what solution would you suggest?
2. How does it come about that a Catholic can grow up without ever having anything to do with a Protestant and vice versa?
3. Does it surprise you that 2 out of 3 parents in Ulster favour integrated schooling for their children?

Contents of the documentary film, part A

Linda had decided to visit Holiday Projects West (HPW) in Londonderry/Derry, where she had arranged to talk to Jerry Tyrrel in the club HPW runs there. She first asked him what had actually brought him there in the first place.

Jerry: I had no connection with Northern Ireland, but I was involved in an organization that ran workcamps. And that particular year, which was 1969 – this was the first time I came here – there was a project involved in... running a play scheme for children.
Now, as I say, I didn't know anything about Northern Ireland. In fact I couldn't even find Londonderry on the map, because the map I had was made in the Irish Republic, and it was down as Derry, not Londonderry. And that's been an issue every since, not with me but with... just generally it's an issue about even what you call this city.
But that first year I worked with children, as I say, on a play scheme just for two weeks. I came back again the following year, worked with the same children. And in the intervening period the army had moved in and it was easy to see the effects of..., the situation was having on the young people. So eventually three of us decided that we wanted to come and live here and get more involved in youth and community work.

Linda then wanted to know how important the youth club where they did the follow-up work after the holidays was to his project. Jerry replied that they saw the work at the club as absolutely vital, as the most important part of the whole year. He explained that the holidays themselves provided a unique opportunity for the children to meet, mix and make friends. The Catholic and Protestant children would not have any other contact otherwise, because they lived in different areas and went to different schools, so that the holiday was a manufactured opportunity for the children to meet. So, he said, they met on holiday and then wanted to meet again afterwards. It was the club that gave them the opportunity.

Jerry told Linda that one way they had of measuring the influence of their work was that quite a few of the volunteers who looked after the children during the holidays had themselves been away as children with HPW during the early seventies. Thus, for example, one of the escorts going with the group to Rostrevor had herself been away as a child. He continued:

> "We see this as maybe one way in which the holiday – which after all is only maybe nine days out of a child's life – does have an effect on them. You probably need to ask other people in the city, but I think it's obvious that, since we have taken something like four or five thousand children away over the last fourteen years, that nearly every family in the city will know of someone. And maybe one of their own members has been away with us. So I would like to think that we have had some effect."

Words

in the first place – in the beginning; *move in* – take control; *follow-up* – something done or an action taken to continue or add to or intensify something done before; *manufactured* – (here) specially created; *volunteer* (n) – a person who offers his/her services willingly or without reward and payment; *escort* (n) /ˈeskɔːt/ – (here) a person who goes on holiday with the children to take care of them and lead them in their activities and games.

Questions

4. On his second visit to Londonderry/Derry Jerry Tyrrel noticed the effects the army's presence was having on the children. Can you suggest what some of these effects were?
5. What were the sort of things that Jerry Tyrrel mentioned which seemed to suggest that Holiday Projects West was having an effect in the western region of Northern Ireland?

*Faith can move mountains

These are the words the Principal used to open the first assembly in the first term of Hazelwood College in September 1985:

> "Ladies, gentlemen and children, we have finally made it. What was a dream less than a year ago is now a reality. Thanks to the tireless efforts of the parents of North Belfast and of the Belfast Charitable Trust for Integrated Education this school has been created. This is no ordinary school and the parents are no ordinary parents. They have put in hundreds of hours' work, soul searching and debate to create this school. They have performed work that no other parents would even dream of.
> Why did they do it?
> There are as many answers as there are parents but one thing I feel that unites them all is faith that this school will do something to create a better future, if not for themselves then for their children and grandchildren. The children of Hazelwood are the children of the dream – the dream of a society where people can live as equals regardless of class, sex or religion. Today is a great beginning to a great future."

Words
the Principal – the head of the school; the headmaster; *assembly* – the meeting of all the teachers and all the children (usually at the beginning of the school day) when they pray together and general announcements are made; *term* – (here) one of the main divisions of time (usually 3 months) into which the school year is divided; *tireless* – never or rarely tired; *trust* (n) – an organization which holds and controls the money for the advantage of others; *soul-searching* – deep examination of one's own mind and conscience.

Question
6. In a certain sense Hazelwood College unites the basic ideals of both Corrymeela and Holiday Projects West. Please outline briefly some of the things they have in common.

B
The Antrim coast

The Giant's Causeway

If one drives from Londonderry/Derry to Belfast, always following the direction of the coast, one covers a little more than 180 miles (some 290 km). It's a winding road, so you need time. However, you really should take your time, since this is considered to be one of the most beautiful coastlines in Europe. At every turn of the road one gets another fine view of the sea, of high cliffs or sandy beaches, or of the lovely **Glens of Antrim**.

Probably the most famous point here is the **Giant's Causeway**, a unique basalt rock formation, often called the 8th Wonder of the World. It was formed some 60 or 70 million years ago, when hot lava burst through the surface of the earth here and slowly cooled. The rocks thus formed are so regular in shape that they look almost man-made. And in fact a legend tells us that a giant used to live here and fell in love with a giantess on one of the Hebrides islands. In order to get to her, he began to build the causeway across the sea which separated him from his loved one...

Here, too, not far from the coast, is the **Old Bushmills Distillery** which claims to be the oldest whiskey distillery in the world. It was founded in 1608.
Perhaps the whiskey here has something to do with it, but the people in the Antrim area are famous for their friendliness. You can easily strike up a conversation here in a pub, but, if you do, make sure you have plenty of time, for the Irish saying tells us, "When God made time, He made plenty of it!"

Words
winding – twisting and turning, with many curves; *coastline* – the shape or outline of a coast (especially as seen from the sea); *cliff* – high, steep face of rock or earth, especially on a coast (Do you remember the White Cliffs of Dover?); *glen* – narrow mountain valley, especially in Scotland and Ireland; *causeway* – a raised road or path especially across wet ground or water; *lava* – rock in a very hot liquid state from an exploding mountain (volcano); *distillery* – factory or place where they make alcoholic spirits; *whiskey* (plural: whiskeys) – the spelling in Ireland and the USA, *whisky* (plural: whiskies) in Scotland and Canada; *He* – please note that whenever we are talking about the one God in English we use capitals for "He", "Him", "His".

Contents of the documentary film, part B

(In this documentary Mr McKay explains how whiskey is made. He uses a number of technical terms which of course you do not need to learn – unless you are particularly interested in how whiskey is produced!)

Linda first travelled along the northern Antrim coast, which is famous for its beauty. Perhaps the most famous spot here is the Giant's Causeway. Not far away is Bushmills Distillery, which claims to be the oldest whiskey distillery in the world. There she was able to talk to Mr McKay, the Production Manager.
Linda wanted to know how they got from spring water to whiskey. He replied that the main ingredients were malted barley, yeast and, of course, water, which is the most important of all.
Mr McKay then went through the various stages in the manufacture of whiskey. First, he said, was the process called mashing. This was intended to extract the sugar out of the malt. The liquor which was then drained from the mash was called wort and when the wort was fermented it became wash. In the next stage, he continued, the fermented wash is distilled in a series of large copper stills. At Bushmills they went through a series of three distillations. After the third distillation they had whiskey. However, he told her that the whiskey was still so strong that it had to be mixed with water and then put into casks in a warehouse for a number of years to mature.
When Linda asked him whether there was a lot of difference between Scotch whisky and Irish whiskey, he answered that the main difference was geographical. Another difference was that Irish whiskey tended not to be as smoky as Scotch whisky. Linda had just one more question she wanted to ask him:

Linda:	Where does the word "whiskey" actually come from?
Mr McKay:	Well, I think the origin of the word "whiskey" is probably in the old word or term "aqua vitae", which meant "the water of life". In Irish this became "uisce beatha", and the English couldn't get their tongues round "uisce beatha" and they just called it whiskey.

The area, however, is not just famous for its coastline and the whiskey. It is also well known for its music and so Linda completed this part of her trip by listening to an Irish band playing typical Irish music in a pub.

Words
ingredients – one of the things needed in a mixture of things; part needed to make something; *malt* – grain kept in water for a time, then dried and used to prepare alcoholic drinks like beer (Malz); *barley* – a grain used to feed both people and cattle, but also used to make beer and spirits (Gerste); *yeast* – a form of small plant life used for producing alcohol in beer and wine and for making bread light and soft (Hefe); *liquor* /ˈlɪkə/ – (strong) alcoholic drink; spirit; *cask* – barrel-shaped container for holding and storing drinks; *warehouse* – cf. unit 28, p.22; *mature* /məˈtjʊə/ (v) – reach an age at which it can be drunk.

*Letter to a Prohibitionist

The second documentary today was intended as a breather during our journey around the U.K., an opportunity for a rest. We were supposed just to sit back and enjoy the Antrim Coast, its friendly people and music – and its whiskey!

Let's continue our rest here by reading a passage by Stephen Leacock (1869-1944). Leacock was a Canadian humorist and satirist who, as he used to say himself, was also a Professor of Economics in his spare time. What he is writing about here is on the subject of alcohol; with tongue in cheek he is writing a letter "to a Prohibitionist", and pretending to approve of the whole idea of Prohibition. Our breather here today then is also an introduction to Anglo-Saxon humour.
The Prohibition was a period of 14 years in the USA, between 1919 and 1933, when it was forbidden to make, sell, or even transport alcoholic beverages. Alcohol and the barroom or saloon were seen as the root of all crime and immorality. However, far from improving things, the illegal sale of alcohol became big business, organized crime increased (think here of Al Capone), and the police force got a bad reputation because too many policemen were corrupt and turned a blind eye to people breaking the law on alcohol.
Now just sit back and enjoy the humour as you read Stephen Leacock's thoughts on the Prohibition.

My dear Sir!

Before I begin this letter let me explain that, of course, I am myself a believer in prohibition. I think that water, especially clear, cold water – I don't care for muddy water – is a beautiful drink. I had a glass of it the other day, and it seemed wonderfully limpid and transparent – almost like gin.

Moreover, in the town in which I live, my friends and I have seen prohibition in actual operation, and we are all enthusiastic over it. Crime is lessening every day. Murder is becoming almost unknown. Not a single one of my friends was murdered all last summer. The sale of boys' boots had increased a hundred per cent. Some of the boys here have no less than eight or ten pairs. Bank deposits are rising. Credit is expanding, and work is almost ceasing.

These are very gratifying things, and when we look back upon the old days, my friends and I wonder how we could have led the life that we did. I remember that very often in the middle of the morning we used deliberately to go out from our business and drink a glass of lager beer. Why we did this I cannot conceive . . . .

I remember, too, that in the old times in the winter evenings we used to sit around the fire in one another's houses smoking and drinking hot toddy. No doubt you remember the awful stuff. We generally used to make ours with Bourbon whiskey and hot water, with just a dash of rum, with half a dozen lumps of white sugar in it, and with nutmeg powdered over the top. I think we used to put a curled slice of lemon peel into the rotten stuff and then served it in a tall tumbler with a long spoon in it. We used to sit and sup this beastly mixture all evening and carry on a perfectly aimless conversation with no selected subject of discussion, and with absolutely no attempt to improve our minds at all.

As things are now I have entirely cut all such idle acquaintanceship and such waste of time. I like to go home after my work and, after drinking four or five glasses of water, spending the evening with some good book of statistics, improving myself. I am then ready to converse, should an occasion arise, in such a way as to put conversation where it ought to be.

You will, therefore, readily understand that all my friends and I are enthusiastic over prohibition. If you were to ask us to go back to things as they were (but please do not do so), we should vote against it by two hundred per cent. It is on this account, with all the more confidence, that I am able to draw your attention to one or two points, in themselves very small things, in which we think that the present regime might be amended.

The first of these is the mere precentage, as it is commonly called, of the beer that is permitted to be sold. This is evidently a matter of very secondary concern and one on which no one would wish to dogmatize. But my friends and I feel that this percentage might profitably be placed at about, say, in rough numbers – twenty per cent. We should feel that at twenty per cent we were getting a more adequate return upon the money expended. At the same time we lay no great stress on the particular figure itself. Twenty, thirty, or possibly still better, forty per cent would prove quite acceptable to us.

Another point is the abolition of the bar. Here we are all agreed. The bar is done with forever. We never want to see it back. But we do feel that if we could have some quiet place where one could purchase beverages of the kind I have described, some plain room with tables and seat or two and possibly a free lunch counter and a weighing machine, we should feel better able to carry out the general purport of the prohibition idea. There are several of my friends who have not been weighed since the first of July of 1919, and are suffering grave inconvenience thereby.

I do not suggest that such a place should be allowed to do business after the old unrestrained fashion of the bars that kept open practically all night. It should be placed under sharp regulation. My friends and I feel that any such place should be rigidly closed at two o'clock a.m. with perhaps special facilities for access at a later hour to the weighing machine and the lunch counter. These, however, are mere details of organization which, as we see it, do not in the least impair the general principle.

As to whiskey and the stronger spirits, we feel that there is not a single word to be said for them. My friends and I are convinced that the use of these things as a beverage is deleterious to the last degree. We unite in declaring that they should be regarded as medicine and as medicine only. Two or three small incidents have occurred among us lately which have corroborated our opinions upon this point. Not very long ago one of my friends was taken, just outside of my door, with a very sharp pain, or stitch, in his side. For the moment I was at a loss what to do when it occurred to me that possibly a medicinal application of whiskey might prove effective. I took him into my house and administered it at once and was delighted to observe the color come back into his cheeks. It was some hours before I was enabled to remove him: but I finally ventured to put him into a hack, crosswise on the two seats, and the poor fellow was, I believe, safely delivered against his own door by the hackman without further ado.

Such incidents as this have convinced us that the sale of whiskey should be rigidly restricted to those who need it at the time when they need it, and in the quantity they happen to need.

These suggestions, my dear sir, are intended merely as suggestions, as mere adumbrations of possible modifications of the present system. We understand that there is some talk of reconsidering and redrafting the eighteenth amendment to the constitution. If this is so, I think it would be well to embody these suggestions in the new amendment. I am certain that upon these terms the Supreme Court of the United States would have no trouble with its interpretation.

(From: Stephen Leacock, *Laugh with Leacock. An Anthology of the Best Work of Stephen Leacock.* McClelland and Stewart Ltd. Toronto/Montreal 1968.)

Words
breather – a short pause for a rest; *with tongue in cheek* – saying something with a serious face which is not intended to be taken seriously; *corrupt* – dishonest; willing to give favours in return for money or other help; *turn a blind eye* – take no notice of something; pretend not to see something (here: pretend not to see that the law has been broken); *limpid* – clear, especially of liquids; *deposit* (n) – money placed in a bank; *gratifying* – giving pleasure, satisfying; *hot toddy* – a sweetened drink of whiskey and hot water; *nutmeg* – a South Pacific nut used as a spice (Muskatnuß); *peel* (n) – the outer covering of some fruit, like oranges and lemons; *tumbler* – a flat-bottomed drinking glass with no handle or stem; *idle* – lazy; here: not useful, producing nothing good; *carry out* – fulfil, complete; *purport* (n) – the general meaning or intention; *unrestrained* – not held back, not reduced; *deleterious* – having a harmful effect; *unite* /juːˈnaɪt/ – act together for a purpose; *stitch* (n) – sharp pain in the side, especially after running; *hack* – (American and Canadian English) a taxi; *hackman* – taxi driver; *adumbration* – incomplete or faint idea of something.

Question
7. Give several examples of what Stephen Leacock says that make it quite clear to the reader that he's being ironical.

C
Focus on language: Indirect speech

We had a look at the Past and Present Perfect Tenses in unit 28, so let's practise indirect speech today.

You remember that, when the reporting verb is in the Present or Present Perfect Tense, we just take over the tenses used in direct speech without any changes:

"I came to Derry from London 14 years ago."
He says he came to Derry from London 14 years ago.

However, when the reporting verb is in a Past or Past Perfect Tense, we have to shift the verb back and make other small changes as well in indirect speech:

"I came to Derry from London 14 years ago."
He said he had come to Derry from London 14 years before.

Exercises

1. Change the following sentences into indirect speech. Use the reporting verbs given.

   a) "Just generally it's an issue about even what you call this city."
      Jerry told Linda that …
   b) "Some people think the situation is hopeless."
      I'm afraid …
   c) "I had no connection with Northern Ireland."
      Jerry added that …
   d) "We see this work with the youth club as being vital."
      We have always maintained that …
   e) "Where does the word 'whiskey' actually come from?"
      She asked Mr McKay where …
   f) "I'll show you the sights of Belfast."
      Werner Heubeck promised them …
   g) "I think that's enough for today."
      He says …
   h) "On the way to work I was listening to a programme from the local fire station."
      Maureen Gallagher pointed out that …

2. Translate the second paragraph of the text *Faith can move mountains*, starting from "Why did they do it?" to the end (p. 86).

3. Explain the following words and expressions. Use complete sentences.

   a) limpid
   b) I've got the stitch!
   c) a mixed marriage
   d) with no strings attached
   e) make allowances for other people's likes and dislikes.

New enterprises in Scotland   Unit 36

A

Start your own business 🎧

Emma Shipton got her chance through Graduate Enterprise.

This unit deals with some aspects of the **economy in Scotland**, especially with the present state of its trade and industry.

Glasgow /ˈglæsgəʊ/, with some 900,000 inhabitants, is Scotland's largest city. It started to prosper in the 18th century, with a rapidly growing cotton industry and the tobacco trade between America and Europe. In the 19th century it was one of the important centres of the steel and shipbuilding industry. Today, however, Glasgow's economic situation is not much better than that of Birmingham (see unit 31!) or, indeed, most other centres of the iron and steel industry the world over.

Edinburgh /ˈedɪnbərə/, Scotland's capital, is better off, because its economy is based on service industries (banks, insurance businesses, etc.). Next to London, Edinburgh is the city with the largest number of banks in the United Kingdom.

On the whole, however, Scotland's economic situation is worse than England's, as the following table from *Britain 1987, An Official Handbook* will show you.

	England	Scotland	Wales	Northern Ireland
Population (in thousands)	46,956	5,146	2,807	1,578
Gross domestic product (£ per head, 1984)	4,708	4,432	3,975	3,615
Unemployment rate (June, 1986)	11.2%	13.6%	14.2%	18.7%
Average gross weekly earnings (£, all full-time men, April '85)	193.3	189.7	179.1	172.0

But in Scotland they have decided not to accept the situation. They want to regain prosperity. One of the groups which have started to fight for a better economic situation in Scotland is the Scottish Enterprise Foundation (SEF), based on the university of Stirling. They run a programme called **Graduate Enterprise** which encourages young people who have graduated from the universities to start their own businesses..(More about new enterprises in Scotland in part B!)

Words
prosper – become successful and rich; *gross* /grəʊs/ *domestic product* – total sum of the value of goods and services produced (Bruttoinlandseinkommen); *average* /ˈævərɪdʒ/ *gross weekly earnings* – the total sum of what all people earn per week divided by the number of people; *enterprise* – here: a business firm; *graduate* /ˈgrædʒʊeɪt/ (v) – obtain a degree from a university; a person who has graduated is called a *graduate* /ˈgrædʒʊət/ (same word, but different pronunciation!)

Questions
1. Have another look at the table on page 93. What does it tell you about the economic situation in Scotland, as compared to that of the other countries within the U.K.? Try to explain why England is better off, while the situation in Wales and Northern Ireland is worse than in Scotland.
2. Why do graduates need extra help and encouragement from SEF? What do you think?

Contents of the documentary film, part A

Most visitors to Scotland go there for the beauty of its lakes and mountains or in order to enjoy the Edinburgh Festival. Linda's plans were different. She wanted to find out more about Graduate Enterprise. Wendy Faulkner, who does research work for the Scottish Enterprise Foundation, first introduced her to Emma Shipton. Emma knew exactly what she wanted to do at a very early age. This is what she told Linda:

> "Well, when I was 14, I decided that I was going to start my own business, because I was too independent to be employed by anybody else. I went to Art College and got my degree in stained glass.
> And then I went on to the Graduate Enterprise course and learnt on the course that there was a market for stained glass in the business community.
> And so I then started up what we have here, my business."

All Graduate Enterprise had to do in Emma's case was to tell her that a great number of people are interested in buying windows or lamp shades made of stained glass – either for their private homes or for the entrance halls and conference rooms of their firms – and that, therefore, it was a good idea for her to start her own business, AURORA GLASS. Emma had learned how to design and work with stained glass at Art College. What she still needed to learn from Graduate Enterprise was how to calculate prices and whatever else a businesswoman has to know in order to run her firm successfully.

At Emma's place, Linda has a good look at a large glass panel on to which Emma had "translated" Beethoven's violin concerto into forms and colours. With the help of her partner, Sandy, Emma does a lot of practical things, too. For example, they buy old glass panels, take them apart and fit them together to form lamp shades, according to the wishes of their customers.

Next we see Linda in Glasgow, visiting another graduate, David Shuttleton. David's business is MACKINTOSH FURNITURE AND FRENCH POLISHING, that is he makes, repairs and restores furniture, specializing in furniture designed by the Scottish architect Charles Rennie Mackintosh (1868-1928).

Linda: What kind of furniture is this, David?
David: This is an example of Charles Rennie Mackintosh reproduction furniture.
Linda: Now, who was Charles Rennie Mackintosh?
David: Charles was a Glasgow architect and designer, furniture designer, from the last century.
Linda: What style is it?
David: It is Art Nouveau furniture.
Linda: And the table?
David: It's also designed by Charles Rennie Mackintosh.
Linda: Is there a lot of Mackintosh furniture in Glasgow?
David: There is a fair number. For example, the Willow Tea Room is a tearoom reproduced in the exact style of the eighteen-eighties.
Linda: You mean I can go to the tearoom and drink tea as they did in the eighteen-hundreds!?
David: Yes, yes.

Since the Willow Tea Room is not far away Linda visits it and finds it packed with people enjoying their tea and the late 19th-century atmosphere.
She returns to David's place and finds out that the prices for the tables and chairs he makes are fairly high.

Words

research /rɪˈsɜːtʃ/ (n) – study of a subject so as to learn new facts or scientific laws; *design* /dɪˈzaɪn/ (v) – make a drawing or pattern, draw plans for something; *stained glass* – glass coloured in its production and used e.g. for church windows; *packed* – crowded, full of people; *Art Nouveau* – French/English for the style of arts and architecture in the late 19th and early 20th centuries (German: Jugendstil).

Questions

3. There are some similarities in Emma's and David's businesses. What are they?
4. Emma's and David's products are rather expensive. Can you imagine the reason why? And why do they have a lot of work to do although they ask fairly high prices?

*Are you enterprising?

This question is on a leaflet which is handed out to university students. The following texts from it will tell you more about Graduate Enterprise.

"Who will manage the businesses in Britain in the next 30 years? It is unlikely to be the graduates! Only 500 out of 14,500 graduates will leave college to run a business. That is 0.3 of 1%. In Germany, Japan and the USA it's a different story..."

(There is a diagram added to the text which shows that in the countries named between 55% and 65% of the management are graduates, in the U.K. less than 5%!)

Why Graduate Enterprise?

"Only 10% of new companies are started by people under 30 in the United Kingdom against 30% in the USA. Most kids come out of University with little idea how to earn money, never mind how to raise it! By contrast, most kids in the US come out knowing how to earn money, they're used to moonlighting to raise money for their degrees. The ones who are going to do best are those with a history of moonlighting. I have great faith that Scotland has lots more enterprising young people. Graduate Enterprise has been started to assist them."

(Professor Tom Cannon, Director of SEF – the man who started Graduate Enterprise)

What can Graduate Enterprise do?

Graduate Enterprise provides a unique chance to discover the immense satisfaction – and rewards – that come from managing your own business.

You may not be thinking of running a business just yet, but are you going to be the boss one day? The best bosses are "enterprising" people. The people who want to change things, achieve things not done before, for their own good, and/or the company's good.

Graduate Enterprise shows you the skills you need to be a boss able to start up a business or improve an existing one.

Graduate Enterprise conferences and seminars provide an insight into what it is like to be an entrepreneur.
If you have a proposition there are advisers to assist.
If you want to start a business we will provide a training programme which will stop you falling flat on your face.

Words

leaflet – a small sheet of information, often folded, usually given free to the public; *moonlight* (v) – have a second job in addition to a regular one or to being a full-time student; *provide* /prə'vaɪd/ – supply, give to a person for use; *achieve* /ə'tʃiːv/ – finish successfully, reach a goal as the result of an action; *proposition* /prɒpə'zɪʃən/ – suggestion, a suggested business offer; *fall flat on one's face* – fail to be successful.

B
Silicon Glen 🎧

A new type of factory building in Silicon Glen

Graduate Enterprise is just one example of what SEF does to help Scotland's economy. It also explains to business people that there is not much hope that the old industries which made Britain rich in the 18th and 19th centuries will ever prosper again and that, instead, it is important to look for new, future-oriented industries in order to better the economic situation.

There is no doubt that the electronic industry is one of the industries of the future. Scotland has succeeded in attracting a large number of high technology firms. Most of them are to be found in **Silicon Glen**, a new industrial area situated between Edinburgh and Glasgow, with Livingston as its centre. You will have heard of **Silicon Valley** in California, where there is a tremendous concentration of hi-tech companies which develop and produce all kinds of electronic equipment, from tiny computer elements to complete, fully automated production systems. During the past couple of years a similar concentration of hi-tech firms has taken place in Silicon Glen.

There are a number of reasons which brought so many firms to this area, the main one being that there are no less than seven universities within a radius of 40 miles of Livingston: Edinburgh (2), Glasgow (2), Stirling, St Andrews, and Dundee. They carry out the research which hi-tech firms live on. And they offer a constant supply of highly qualified graduates for them to employ.

Words

silicon /ˈsɪlɪkən/ – a non-metallic substance which is used a lot in the electronic industry; *glen* – Scottish word for "valley"; *technology* – the branch of knowledge dealing with scientific methods and their practical use in industry; *hi-tech* /haɪˈtek/ – short for high technology: a technology dealing with the most advanced methods, especially electronics.

Questions

5. The electronic industry is growing rapidly. Can you name a few examples to show that electronic devices play an important part in everyday life today?
6. What effects does the creation of a large new industrial area like Silicon Glen have on the economy of a country? Are there positive effects only, or can you think of negative ones, too?

Contents of the documentary film, part B

Linda meets Wendy Faulkner again on the campus of Stirling University. She wants to know what Wendy does apart from helping graduates to become their own bosses. So Wendy tells her:

> "Well, I am involved in the research side of the Foundation's activities, and in particular I look at new technology-based firms. These firms are very important to Scotland. As you probably know, we've earned the name of Silicon Glen in the centre of Scotland. And really that refers to the growth of clusters of technology-based firms, and really in the radius surrounded by the large universities of Scotland."

Linda decides to visit Livingston, the capital of Silicon Glen. The first thing she notices is the large number of new houses which all look like big cardboard boxes to her. The other thing that strikes her is that the factories in Livingston look very different from the ones she had seen in the Midlands and in Northern Ireland. She also sees large supermarkets and a great number of buses which take the workers from the neighbouring cities to their jobs in Livingston.

Then Linda visits one of the hi-tech firms – an American company – and talks to its Director, David Wood. David shows her a wafer, which is one of the main products of his firm.

Linda: So this is a wafer. Now what has this wafer got to do with the computer screen?

David: This wafer is made up of many rows of small individual integrated circuits, called chips. The lines on the individual circuits are way too small for us to see with the naked eye. So the designers use this computer to actually blow up some perhaps 250 times the size of the lines on the individual circuit, so that they can place them exactly where they want them, and to make the proper interconnections on the circuit, so that the circuit will work, of course.

Then, what happens after that is that they finish their complete design of the whole circuit, reduce that to a magnetic tape. That magnetic tape then goes to the production facility, and the people in production use the magnetic tape to process the individual wafer and the individual circuits across the wafer, as we see here.

David tells Linda that the chips produced on the wafers are used in typewriters and other office products, but also in military equipment and in electricity grids. Then Linda wants to know what brought David from Silicon Valley in California to Silicon Glen in Scotland. Here is his answer:

> "Well, this company was actually started up by about 10 Americans from the Silicon Valley environment – experts in integrated circuits and some management.
> We decided at the outset of this company that we wanted to serve the European marketplace as well as the American marketplace.
> To serve properly the European marketplace, we have to be inside the EEC, because there are import duties on these kinds of chips into the EEC. Therefore we made that decision.
> Then we began to look for a location and decided on Scotland, primarily because Scotland has the support and infrastructure for our kind of industry..."

Finally Linda asks David how he sees the future of the electronic industry in Britain. David thinks that the prospects are very bright because companies keep moving in to serve this kind of industry. His own firm is growing rapidly, so he can offer more jobs, and about 60% of the firm's sales go back into the USA.

Words

cluster (n) – a number of things of the same kind close together in a group: *cardboard boxes* – boxes made of a thick stiff paperlike material; *wafer* – a very thin cake, here a thin round piece of silicon; *screen* (n) – the front surface of an electronical instrument, like a TV set, showing information; *blow up* – enlarge, make bigger; *import duty* – taxes you have to pay when you bring goods into the country.

(Technical terms are not explained here because those of you who are familiar with computers will understand these terms anyway since they are being used internationally. Those of you who are not particularly interested in computers do not have to understand all the details because, after all, this unit is not a course in electronics. It is about new industries in Scotland.)

Questions
7. In the film you have seen some of the factories in Silicon Glen. In what way are they different from the factories in Birmingham or Belfast?
8. Why did many hi-tech firms settle in Silicon Glen? Give at least two reasons!

*Make it in Livingston – Europe's most logical location

This slogan is on the front page of an information folder which the Livingston Development Corporation hands out in order to attract even more hi-tech firms. The following text from that folder will tell you why people in Livingston think that their town is the best – or, as they call it, the "most logical" – location for international electronic firms which want to settle in Europe.

KIRKTON CAMPUS is Scotland's first, and by far and away, most successful science park... 250 acres of high quality environment land fully laid out and serviced to meet the demands of research-based industry. Europe's most logical location.

• In the heart of Livingston, West Lothian, which itself is at the centre of Scotland's communications system providing an immediate entree to Europe, Kirkton Campus is excellently placed to benefit from close links with Scottish Universities (it has seven within a 40-mile radius and one on its "doorstep"); the industrialised central belt of Scotland and the major administrative and financial centres of Glasgow and Edinburgh. In addition, there are links to the Clyde and Forth and the north-east of Scotland is within easy reach for industry based on North Sea oil support services.

• Livingston Development Corporation, its owners and developers, have made it a fundamental concept of the Campus that the best possible standards of environmental quality buildings, amenity, landscaping, etc., are maintained. It is designed for low density of workers per acre, and all services (electricity, gas, water and telecommunications) have all to be laid underground. Incidentally, energy supplies are plentiful in Livingston and the Scottish water is famous all over the world for its purity.

• On Kirkton Campus science park you will find an environment second to none; good neighbours in practically every facet of industrial activity... and a working environment amidst woodland and footpaths which will encourage the best from your workforce. Obviously Europe's most logical location.

Words

slogan – short phrase expressing a political or advertising message; *serviced to meet the demands* – offering all services which are needed, such as transport, water, electricity, communication systems, etc.; *provide an entree* /'ɒntreɪ/ – give the right or freedom to enter; *benefit from* – gain by, have the advantage of; *amenity* /ə'miːnətɪ/ – conditions in a place which make it pleasant and enjoyable; *low density of workers* – enough space for all so that the workers are not crowded together; *every facet of* – all kinds of.

C
Focus on language: Texture

When we talk of the texture of textiles, e.g. a tablecloth, we are referring to the way in which the threads in the cloth go over and under each other – the way in which they are *interwoven*. You can also talk of the texture of a piece of music or a text – of the way in which various melodies in a sonata or the words and phrases in a speech or conversation are interwoven.

Let us look at Linda's conversation with David Shuttleton again and see how the questions and answers in that interview are interwoven:

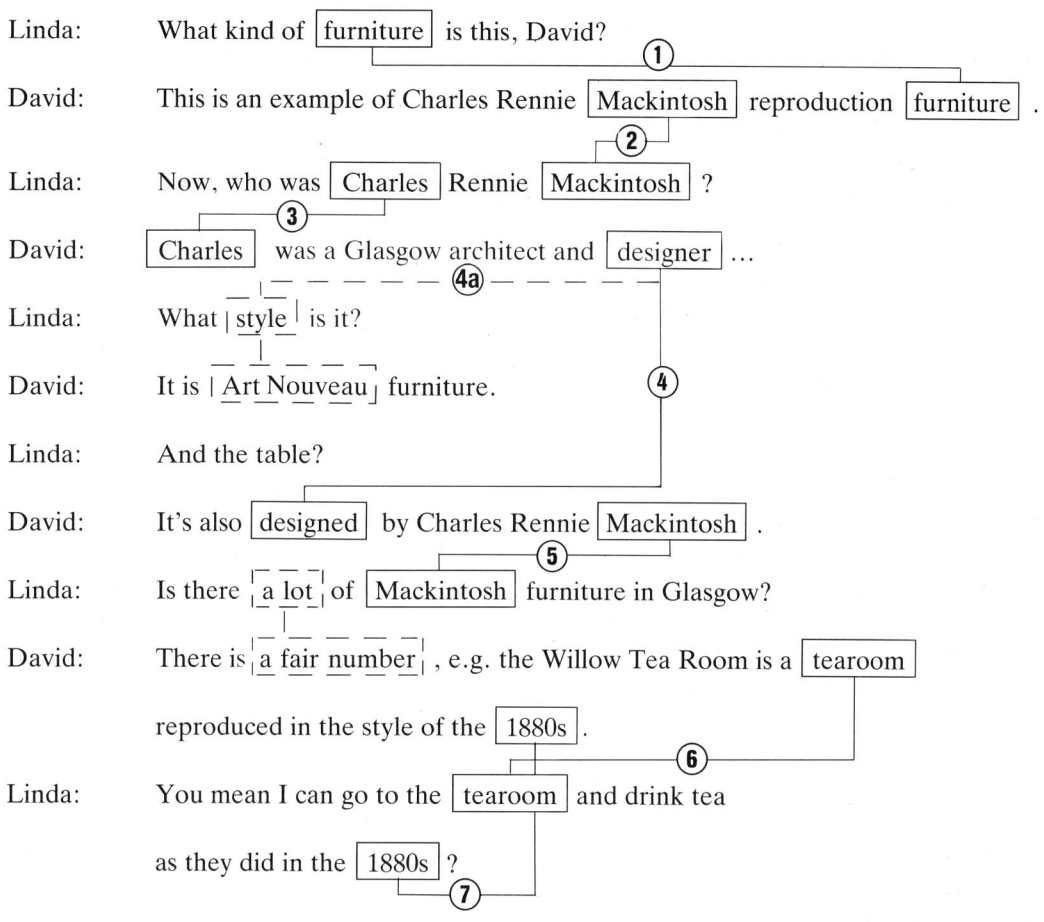

The diagram shows clearly how one person takes up the words of the other person. This kind of texture serves two purposes:

– The interviewer (Linda in our case) makes sure that she has understood the information correctly (here: the name of an architect, a place, and a date).

– The interviewer uses the information picked up from the answer in her next question. By this she shows that she wants more information on the same subject. ("Who was...?")

A good texture of repetition of words and phrases is particularly helpful in situations of communication in which one person is the expert, the other person a non-expert. In such situations repetitions help the non-expert to understand words – especially technical terms –, names, dates and facts which are new to him.

Exercises

1. A typical example of a situation in which person A wants to pass knowledge or information to person B (or person B wants to learn something from person A) is the classroom situation. Find more examples. List them like this:

expert	non-expert	situation
teacher	*pupil(s)*	*classroom*

2. When David Wood explained the production process in his firm to Linda, he gave his explanations a good textural structure. He knew that Linda was not an expert in microelectronics. In order to make sure that Linda could follow his explanations he used a lot of words more than once.
   Here are his explanations once again. Their texture will make it easy for you to fill in the missing words.

   > "Now what has this wafer got to do with the computer screen?"
   > "This … is made up of integrated circuits.
   > The lines on the individual … are way too small for us to see. So the designers use this … to blow up the lines on the … They reduce the design of the whole … to a magnetic tape. That … then goes to the production facility.
   > And the people in … use the … to process the wafer and the circuits across the …"

3. Tell a visitor from the U.K. what TELEKOLLEG is and how you learn with it. Remember that all you tell him will be new to him. So try to follow David's example by giving your explanation a good textural structure!

4. Translate into German
   a) the dialogue between Linda and David Shuttleton from the contents of part A;
   b) David Wood's explanation of the production of chips from the contents of part B.
   In each case, try to show the texture of the texts in your translation!

The Athens of the North
Britons by the Sea

Unit 37

Most people who travel to foreign countries for their holidays choose nice places to stay in. They want to enjoy a beautiful landscape or get a good suntan. Linda did different things during most of her time in the U.K.: She tried to find out – for herself and for you – how people live in the U.K. today, what they do, what they are interested in, what the country's economic situation is like, what changes are taking place, etc. In this unit, however, Linda takes a breather – a short pause for a rest – and joins the tourists and holidaymakers, first in Edinburgh, then on the coast in the northeast of England.

A

Edinburgh – the Athens of the North

Edinburgh, the Athens of the North

You know a few things about Edinburgh already. It is Scotland's capital and, next to London, the most important financial centre in the U.K., with international banks and insurance companies, and a large number of shops and department stores.
The city is situated in the valley of the River Leith and on the rolling hills which surround it. On one of the hills, which is a massive volcanic rock, there is the **Castle**, the first home of the kings of Scotland. Down from the Castle there are four streets in one line; they form what is known as the **Royal Mile**. It runs through the oldest parts of the city where there are many historic buildings and narrow lanes called "closes". At the far end of the Royal Mile you get to the royal palace of

Holyrood House, built about the year 1500 and re-built, after destruction, in 1671–1679. The newer part of the city lies north of **Princes Street**, which is the widest and best known of the elegant streets and squares which are laid out like a chess-board.

Edinburgh is known as the **Athens of the North**. Because of its situation on and among hills and because of its fine architecture it is considered to be one of the most beautiful capital cities north of the Alps. Some Scottish authors and architects of the 19th century found that the city had a great resemblance to Athens in Greece. One of them, the publisher Robert Chambers (1802-1871) wrote in his *Walkes of Edinburgh*: "...the landscape is exactly that of the vicinity of Athens." He likens the Castle to the Acropolis, and the Firth of Forth, which is to the northwest of the city, to the Aegean sea, and he says that "the hills of the Peloponnese are precisely those of the opposite coast of Fife". A number of buildings which are copies of ancient Greek monuments and temples help to make Edinburgh look even more like Athens. The most impressive of these "Greek" buildings is a copy of the Parthenon on Calton Hill. It was to be a national monument to those Scots who lost their lives in the wars fought against Napoleon. It was, however, never finished.

Edinburgh was, and still is, one of Europe's most important cultural centres – again just as Athens was the cultural centre of the Ancient World. There are two universities in the city, and a number of museums, art galleries, academies, libraries, and theatres. The **Edinburgh International Festival of Music and Drama** brings artists and guests to the city from all over the world each year.

Words

destruction /dɪˈstrʌkʃən/ – the act of tearing down or destroying something; *resemblance* – likeness; *vicinity* – surroundings; *liken to* – compare with; *ancient* /ˈeɪnʃənt／ – of times long ago.

Questions
1. Why is Edinburgh called the Athens of the North? Give at least two reasons.
2. What kind of people go to Edinburgh – and for what reasons?

Contents of the documentary film, part A

Linda's tour of Edinburgh first takes her to a park. Here she meets Allan Porteous, an artist and teacher, who is sketching what looks like a small Greek temple: St Bernard's Well. He shows Linda some more sketches he has done of the city and its surroundings. Some of them show buildings and monuments on Calton Hill:

- the copy of the Parthenon (which Allan calls "Edinburgh's Disgrace", because it was never finished as the city ran out of money);
- Nelson's memorial, which is in the shape of a telescope;
- the memorial of the Scottish poet and philosopher Dugald Stewart (1749–1822);
- the Royal Observatory, one of the oldest planetariums in the world.

There are also sketches of streets in Edinburgh and of places just outside the city, like

- Swanston Village – a small and quiet village where Robert Louis Stevenson lived for three years (Stevenson, 1850–1894, wrote books like *Treasure Island* and *Dr Jekyll and Mr Hyde*, which are well known even today.);
- the 15th century Roslin Chapel with its rich stone carvings.

At the end of this "sightseeing tour" Linda tells Allan:

Linda:	Thanks, that was marvellous. That's what I call a quick tour of a town.
Allan:	Well, we've really only just scratched the surface. You must go and look at the things.
Linda:	I think I'll do that now.
Allan:	I could take you, but it'll cost you a drink!
Linda:	You are Scottish, aren't you?
Allan:	What do you expect in Scotland?

So they visit all the places Linda has first seen in Allan's sketchbook. Afterwards Linda wants to buy something typically Scottish. She goes to a store where they sell pullovers, cardigans, and shawls, most of them knitted of pure Scottish wool – the more expensive ones being handknitted. When Linda meets Allan again at a pub, she cannot buy him a drink because she is broke, having spent all her money on woollens. So Allan decides that the drinks will be on him.

Words
disgrace – shame, loss of honour and respect; *carving* – something made by cutting wood or stone to make a special shape; *cardigan* – short woollen coat with sleeves, but without collar and fastened at the front with buttons; *broke* – completely without money; *woollens* – garments made of wool; *this is on me* – I will pay for it.

Questions
3. Tell in a few sentences what you know about Nelson, whose memorial is on Calton Hill.
4. Do you know of copies of Greek buildings in Germany?

*Impressions of a city

The first two of the following short texts will give you an idea why many people feel that Edinburgh is a city with a very special atmosphere. The third text will tell you what the city is like during the Festival.

"One afternoon in December 1944 two of us were sitting at an upstairs window of a Princes Street tea-room as the winter dusk was falling and the Castle grew dark and mysterious on its high rock. 'Mine own romantic town', murmured my companion, quoting Scott's famous phrase about his native city. It was wartime, and when darkness fell on the street below it was unrelieved. Years later they took to flood-lighting the Castle and visitors to the Edinburgh Festival looked up in admiration at the impossible fairy-tale building floating in white light above the city. Dark or shining, that Edinburgh scene can always be counted on to arouse emotion..."
(From: David Daiches, *Edinburgh*. Ebenezer Bylis & Son Ltd., London 1978, p.8.)

"To emerge from Waverley Station as a newcomer to Edinburgh and see, high above one on the left, the spiky skyline of the buildings on the old town ridge dominated by the Castle on its rock, with ahead the classical outlines of the Royal Scottish Academy Gallery and the Scottish National Gallery over the green hollow of East Princes Street Gardens, and on the right the spire of the Walter Scott Monument, gothic and ornate, towering over Princes Street – can there be, anywhere else, so dramatic an introduction to a city and one that comprehends, in a single glance, so much of a city's history?"

(From: E.F. Catford, *Edinburgh. The story of a city*. The Anchor Press Ltd., London 1975, p.11.)

"For three weeks every summer, Edinburgh is alive with exhilarated festival-goers and performers who come from all over the world, and the city is gay with flags and decorations. This international festival of the arts fills every theatre, concert hall, exhibition gallery and assembly room with performances of opera, dancing, music, plays, revues, films, puppet shows and recitals, and specially-mounted exhibitions of painting and sculpture. The festival is not limited to indoor activities: every weekday the noise of the city's traffic is lost in the sound of music as the Scottish pipers march along Princes Street with kilts swinging and drums beating. But the most spectacular event of the festival is undoubtedly the military tattoo. This takes place under searchlights on the Castle esplanade – the scene of many executions in the past – with the floodlit castle in the background. Nowhere could you find a natural setting more impressive and appropriate."

(From: M.D. Munro Mackenzie & L.J. Westwood, *Background to Britain*. The Macmillan Press Ltd., London & Basingstoke 1978, p.70.)

Words

unrelieved – not varied, unchanged (In wartime, no lights were allowed in the open to lighten the streets.); *impossible* – here: hard to believe; *floating* – here: held up in the air as if by magic (because the castle rock is in darkness and therefore not visible to the spectator); *arouse* – cause to wake, bring into being; *emerge* /ɪ'mɜːdʒ/ – come or appear from somewhere; *spiky* /'spaɪkɪ/ – having sharp points; *ridge* /rɪdʒ/ – top of a range of hills or mountains; *spire* /'spaɪə/ – roof rising steeply to a point on top of a building; *gothic* – here: a style of building common in Europe in the Middle Ages; *ornate* – having a great deal of ornament; *exhilarated* /ɪɡ'zɪləreɪtəd/ – cheerful and excited; *recital* /rɪ'saɪtl/ – performance of poetry or music; *tattoo* /tæ'tuː/ – an outdoor military show with music, usually in the late evening.

B
Britons by the Sea – How it all began

In the middle of the 18th century, a doctor from Sussex made it known to the public that sea water was healthy to drink and to bathe in. This brought large numbers of rich and fashionable ladies and gentlemen to the seaside. They needed hotels, and they wanted to be entertained after their bath in the sea. As a result, small fishing villages were turned into elegant seaside resorts, with hotels, theatres, pleasure piers and hundreds of "bathing-machines". These were little huts on wheels which were drawn down into the sea, so that the bathers could undress and get into the water without being seen by the public. (The bathing costume had not been invented at that time!)

A rainy day at Robin Hood's Bay

A pier is a bridgelike framework built out into the sea at which boats can stop to take on or land their passengers and goods. During the reign of Queen Victoria piers were also built for pleasure. They were elegant structures with buildings on them, some of them looking almost like a palace. Here people could go to eat and drink and amuse themselves. Altogether some one hundred pleasure piers were built in those days.

Things have changed a lot since then. Many piers have been washed away by rough seas or were bombed during World War II. Others were not kept in good repair for lack of money, since many people began to prefer holiday places abroad where one can be sure to have sunshine day after day. So, today, it is mostly poorer people, who cannot afford to take their families to southern countries and therefore spend their holidays by their own country's seaside. And they go there in large numbers. **Brighton**, for example, England's largest and best known seaside resort on the south coast, has been given the nickname "London by the Sea", because Londoners go there by their thousands for their holidays or just for a weekend. Another well-known British seaside resort is **Blackpool**, on the west coast of England. That is where people from the Midlands and the North go. But, of course, there are a whole lot of smaller resorts on Britain's long coastline.

(Adapted from: Elizabeth Gundrey, *England by the Sea*. Severn House Publishers Ltd., London 1982, pp.56,59.)

Words

fashionable /ˈfæʃnəbl/ – dressed after the latest fashion; *resort* /rɪˈzɔːt/ – holiday place or place considered good for the health; *framework* – that part of a structure that gives shape and support; *afford* /əˈfɔːd/ – be able to spend money.

Questions
5. What is the longest distance from any place in Britain to the sea? (Have a look at a map of the British Isles!)
6. Why are there many places for amusement at British seaside resorts?

Contents of the documentary film, part B

On her way from Scotland back to England Linda stops at Robin Hood's Bay, a small seaside resort on the east coast. It is a cold, wet and windy day, and yet there are many holidaymakers on the rocky beach, enjoying themselves despite the bad weather. A lot of them are in their summer clothes, too – shorts and sandals, for example – and some are in the shallow water, with bare feet, looking for pebbles and seashells.

Linda decides that it is too cold for her on the beach. She takes a walk through the narrow streets of the village. Many of them are rather like staircases leading up and down the steep hill on which Robin Hood's Bay is built. She sees that a lot of the old houses and cottages are let to holidaymakers.

In the village she meets Joe Green, whom she mistakes for an American. Here is some of their conversation:

Joe:	Well, hi there. How are y'all?
Linda:	American?
Joe:	Definitely not.
Linda:	You could have fooled me.
Joe:	Yes, well, I live there now, but originally I come from around here.
Linda:	Oh! – Well, what are you doing here?
Joe:	Oh, just taking a little vacation, visiting family. And you?
Linda:	Well, I'm doing some research for school.
Joe:	Research for school, hm?
Linda:	Well, if you're from here, maybe you could tell me why this place is called Robin Hood's Bay.
Joe:	Ah, if you ask 10 different people, you'll get 10 different answers to that one. But the one that I know is that Robin Hood needed to have some place to go when things got really hot,... when the Sheriff of Nottingham was chasing after him. – You have heard of the Sheriff of Nottingham, I presume? – And Robin Hood? – O.K. So, the story goes that he came through the woods and over the moors, which are down there, and hid out here in Robin Hood's Bay. He even kept a couple of boats to be able to get off shore.
Linda:	So it sounds like Robin Hood's getaway!?
Joe:	Well, I am not sure where he got away to. Maybe he took his boats up the coast to Whitby, which is a few miles north of here. Uh, you ever been to Whitby?
Linda:	No, I haven't.

Linda takes Joe's advice and goes to Whitby. Before she meets Joe again (as you will see in unit 38!), she has another good look at Britons by the Sea. The weather is not much different from what it was the previous day, but for British holidaymakers it is summer, whether the sun shines or not. Whitby has a lot more to offer than Robin Hood's Bay: There is a long sandy beach there, and a promenade where you can sit and look down on the sands. These amusements are free, but there is also ample opportunity to spend money – in the Bingo halls and at the slot machines, at the fortune teller's, in Count Dracula's place, or for a round of crazy golf. There is also a funfair there for the kids. Of the many small restaurants, people seem to like the fish and chips shops best.

NOTE: It is true that Linda did not experience many sunny days during her tour of the U.K. But the British weather is not as bad as the Britons themselves make us believe. If you are lucky you can have a nice warm summer on the British Isles, and if you are unlucky you can have a cool and rainy summer in Germany!

Words
pebbles – small smooth stones; *seashells* – shells of small sea animals (e.g. mussels) as found on the shore; *mistake for* – think wrongly that somebody is someone else; *fool someone* – deceive somebody; *get hot* – here: get dangerous; *getaway* – an escape, a place you can run away to and hide in; *slot machine* – machine for selling drinks, cigarettes, etc.; also a machine into which people put money to try and win more money (Some of these machines have a long handle and are therefore nicknamed "one-armed bandits".); *crazy golf* – (German: Minigolf); *funfair* – place with merry-go-rounds and other machines to ride on, games of skill, and other amusements.

Question
7. Compare the life at a British seaside resort with a German one. What are the differences, and what do they have in common?

*Another look at British seaside resorts

"No town in Britain is more than eighty miles from the sea and there are seaside resorts all round the coast. On a summer Sunday most of the roads that lead to the sea are congested with cars full of people eager to get a breath of sea air. Once at the beaches, the children hasten to unload their buckets and spades and start to build sandcastles or paddle in the shallow water. Father may go for a swim or sit and doze in his deck-chair while mother knits. In the evening when everyone is full of food, ice-cream and rock, there is the long, slow drive home on roads crowded with returning cars...

For most Britons 'holiday' and 'seaside holiday' mean one and the same thing and, in the last fifty years or so, 'resorts' of every kind have sprung up to cater to the Englishman's need to spend a part of the year, however briefly, by the seaside. Of course, many British people go abroad for their holidays, and package tours to warmer countries are very popular with those who can afford them."

(From: M.D. Munro Mackenzie & L.J. Westwood, *Background to Britain*. The Macmillan Press Ltd., London & Basingstoke 1978, p.62.)

Words
rock – here: a hard sweet in the form of a long stick.

C
Focus on language: Ellipsis

Ellipsis /ɪ'lɪpsɪs/ is a grammatical term which simply means the leaving out of a word or words from a sentence when the meaning can be understood without them. Here is an example:

Remember what I told you yesterday?

The full sentence would, of course, read:

<u>Do you</u> remember what I told you yesterday?

We all use ellipsis a lot in spoken language when we are talking about *everyday things*. We do not want to repeat certain words over and over again when there is no need to do so.

Exercises

1. Have another look at Joe's and Linda's conversation on page 108. Fill in the words they have left out – but only in the shortened sentences, of course!

2. Let us try the other way round, now! Shorten the following sentences! (Remember that you can also shorten words by leaving out a letter or a group of letters, e.g. *that is* to *that's* or *he will* to *he'll*, etc.)

   "What do you think about going down to the beach today?" – "I think that is a good idea." – "At what time shall we go down?" – "Let us go there at eleven o'clock." – "Eleven o'clock is a bit late. Can we not go at ten o'clock?" – "I am sorry, but I would like to finish these letters first." – "All right, we will go at eleven o'clock, then."

After you have finished exercise 1 you will see that your long version of the conversation does not carry any more information than the original short version. On the other hand, you will see that, in exercise 2, the long version with all its repetitions sounds rather artificial and that your short version represents the way we really talk to each other.

When Tim Brown (unit 33) or David Wood (unit 36) talked to Linda, the situation was very different. They were *not* talking about things Linda was familiar with. Tim and David were *experts, talking to a non-expert*. So they did not use ellipsis. Instead, they used long forms and even repeated new expressions a couple of times, in order to make things clear to Linda.

In other words: You can and should use ellipsis, that is shorten your sentences, whenever it is possible. The British do it a lot in conversation, as you will have noticed in our documentary films. However, avoid ellipsis when you have to explain difficult things to someone who is not familiar with what you are talking about.

3. Turn the contents of part A into a report given by Linda herself. Start like this: "My tour of Edinburgh first took me to a park..."
   (Note that you have to make two changes: from third to first person singular, and from present to past tense! – You may leave out the descriptions of the buildings and monuments in and around Edinburgh.)

Fishermen and farmers — Unit 38

A

Whitby – the past and the present 🎧

Whitby, past and present

In this unit we will have a look at the United Kingdom's **agriculture** and **fishing industry**. In order to find out what the situation is today in those two fields of the economy, Linda talked to fishermen in Whitby and to farmers in North Yorkshire. Whitby is not only an important fishing harbour and a place where many British people spend their summer holidays (see unit 37!), it is also famous for its abbey. The story of **Whitby Abbey** tells us quite a bit about an important chapter in the history of the whole country.

Whitby is situated at the mouth of the River Esk. Its bed cuts into the surrounding high cliffs. Whitby Abbey is on the eastern cliff, overlooking the sea and the harbour. It was founded as early as 657 AD and played an important role in establishing the Roman Christian church in England. In 851 it was destroyed by the Vikings and refounded shortly after the Norman conquest (1066). From the 12th to the 15th century a magnificent church was built of which now only ruins are left.

Why is Whitby Abbey a ruin today? The answer to this question takes us back to the reign of King Henry VIII (1509–47). As a young man he had defended Catholicism against Martin Luther and the Reformation. This is why the Pope gave him the title *Defender of the Faith*. (To this day the kings and queens of England use this title. You can even read it on the coins: F.D., which is short for "Fidei Defensor", the Latin form of that title). When, however, Henry VIII wanted to divorce his first wife, because they had no son, the Pope refused to give his permission. So Henry broke with

Rome and closed the monasteries. With the monks and nuns driven out of their houses, there was nobody there to keep the churches and monastery buildings in repair. They became ruins. In some instances, people even used them as quarries: they took stones from the buildings and used them for their own houses.

Since the late 19th century there are two associations in the U.K. which will no longer allow that places of historic interest or natural beauty are destroyed – as was Whitby Abbey. These are the **National Trust** (covering England, Wales and Northern Ireland) and the **National Trust for Scotland**. The two trusts together have a membership of more than 1.2 million people. Most of the money the trusts need to keep up old churches, castles, etc. or places of natural beauty comes from their members; the regular fee is £ 12.50 per person and year (1983). The trusts are a good example of the British peoples' interest in preserving their national heritage.

For England, there is yet another society which keeps up places of historic interest. It is called **English Heritage** (Historic Buildings & Monuments Commission for England). Throughout England, English Heritage cares for over 350 historic buildings and monuments, from prehistoric and Roman remains, to industrial buildings, castles, country houses and abbeys.

Words

abbey /ˈæbɪ/ – a monastery with an abbot as the head of the religious community; *conquest* – the act of taking (land) by force; *faith* – here: belief and trust in God; *Defender of the Faith* – one who keeps Christianity safe from harm; *quarry* – (see unit 33, p. 66.); *heritage* /ˈherɪtɪdʒ/ – something which one receives from an older member of the family.

Questions

1. As you have read in the first chapter of this unit, Henry VIII split from Rome and drove the Roman Catholic monks and nuns out of their houses. All the people in his kingdom had to join the Church of England. – Today, everyone in Britain has the right of religious freedom. That includes, of course, Roman Catholics. There are some 5.7 million of them in the U.K. now. Have you any idea where they came from? (Remember what we said about the miners in the south of Wales – unit 33 – and what you have learned about Northern Ireland – units 34/35!)
2. Whitby Abbey is an English Heritage property now. Some other places you have seen in our films are kept in good repair by the National Trust or English Heritage. Can you name two of them?
3. Who looks after places of historic interest and natural beauty in the Federal Republic of Germany?

Contents of the documentary film, part A

In Whitby, Linda climbs up the 199 steps to the Abbey. At the top of the stairs she meets Joe Green again. Here is some of the first part of the conversation they have as they walk through an old churchyard towards the Abbey:

Linda:	Joe, yesterday you mentioned that this place was full of lore and legend.	
Joe:	Yeah, that's right. They say that even Dracula came here.	
Linda:	Come on!	

Joe:	No, in Bram Stoker's book, if you've read his book, *Count Dracula*, ships sailed up a river with a dog on it. And the dog jumped off the ship and transformed into Dracula at night. And that was actually based here in Whitby. You see there, the harbour mouth?
Linda:	Yes.
Joe:	That points due north into what used to be called the German Ocean.
Linda:	You mean the North Sea was called the German Ocean?
Joe:	Yeah, up to about 70 years ago.
Linda:	Why was that changed?
Joe:	Oh, well, the First World War, and the English didn't like calling it that any more, so they changed it.

As they walk through the Abbey, Joe tells Linda about Henry VIII and his splitting from Rome, in order to explain to her why the Abbey is in ruins. He even shows her a house nearby which was built from stones taken from the old church building. Then Joe takes Linda down to the harbour. Linda wants to know what it is like for him to come back to the town of his boyhood, after all those years in the USA. Are things a lot different nowadays, she wonders? Here is Joe's reply:

> "Oh, they are not a lot different, because in a town like this, which is so old, everything changes very, very slowly.
> But I think, if there was one thing that I would notice more than anything else, especially at this time of year, . . . it's the fishing boats. 25 years ago the harbour would have been full of herring boats.
> I mean, like there'd have been six across, just waiting to offload their herring, go back out to sea and catch more fish. But off shore, waiting to come into the harbour, you'd have even more boats."

Joe tells Linda, if she wants to learn more about the fishing industry, she should see his old friend Arthur Coulson.

Linda meets Arthur at a fish auction. Later on, at the far end of the harbour pier, Linda asks him:

Linda:	Joe Green told me that 25 years ago you could walk across the harbour on fishing boats. Today there don't seem to be that many here.
Arthur:	Yes, that was a fact. 25 years ago in Whitby we had a huge herring fleet that came from other ports, mainly Scottish ports, during the summer months. And you were able to walk across those vessels at high tide without getting your feet wet from one side of Whitby Harbour to the other. But I am afraid the shoals of herring were decimated, and the fleets could no longer come down here to make a living. It was impossible.
Linda:	Has Britain's joining the EEC made things here more difficult for you?

Arthur:	No, not difficult. We welcome the transition from non-legislation to European legislation. Local legislation safeguarded our own fleet only, but the European legislation which was brought in safeguarded the stocks as a whole in the North Sea. And the decimation of the shoals of fish which was taking place is now getting smaller.
Linda:	But there's lots of talk about pollution in the North Sea. Is it affecting the fish?
Arthur:	Ah, it doesn't affect me and I swim in the North Sea! No, it doesn't affect the fish, not in this part of the North Sea. The pollution is very, very low indeed. We have a very clean sea.

Words

lore and legend – old folk tales and tradition (folklore!); *transformed into* – changed into; *vessel* – ship or large boat; *shoal* or *school* of herring – a large group of herring swimming together; *decimate* /'desɪmeɪt/ – destroy a large number of (fish); *safeguard* – protect; *stock* – here: supply of fish.

*The British Fishing Industry and the European Economic Community (EEC)

"Britain is one of Europe's most important fishing nations. The fishing industry provides about 66 per cent of British fish supplies, and is an important source of employment and income in a number of ports. In 1985 there were 16,150 fishermen in regular employment and nearly 5,800 occasionally employed. The Government aims to encourage the development of a viable, efficient and market-orientated fisheries industry within the framework of the European Community's Common Fisheries Policy. The main concerns of government fisheries policy are conservation and exploitation of sea fish stocks, financial support for fleet modernisation..., the improvement of the industry's technical and economic performance,... and protection of the aquatic environment. Community countries, and certain non-Community countries having fishery agreements with the Community, may fish up to Britain's 12-mile limit... With the extension of fishery limits to 200 miles in the mid-1970s, new arrangements became necessary to control Community fishing in the greatly extended area. Britain has a particularly strong interest in such control, since a sizeable proportion of the total catch within the 200-mile limits of member states is taken in British waters..."

People employed (June 1985) in
- agriculture, forestry and fishing — 1.6%
- energy and water supply — 2.9%
- manufacturing — 25.8%
- construction (of houses, bridges ...) — 4.5%
- service industries — 65.3%

Total catch by British fishing vessels — 760,000 tonnes

(Text and statistics from: *Britain 1987. An official handbook.*)

Words

aim to – intend to, direct one's efforts to; *viable* /ˈvaɪəbl/ – able to succeed in operation; *concern* /kənˈsɜːn/ (n) – a matter that is of interest or importance to someone; *exploit* /ɪkˈsplɔɪt/ – use or develop (a thing) fully so as to get profit; *aquatic* /əˈkwætɪk/ *environment* – living conditions in the water; *sizeable* /ˈsaɪzəbl/ – fairly large.

Questions
4. What makes Britain "one of Europe's most important fishing nations"?
5. Still, only 1.6% of all people employed in Britain work in the fishing industry *and* in agriculture and forestry. Can you offer any reasons for this comparatively small percentage?
6. In what way does Britain's fishing industry benefit from Britain's membership in the EEC?

B
Traditional farming – modern farming

Norman Stockdale's traditional farm

In the United Kingdom about 75 per cent of the land area is used for agriculture. Some twelve million hectares (30 million acres) are under crop and grass. In hill country, some six million hectares are also used for rough grazing (sheep, cattle). Soils in the highlands are fairly thin poor ones. In low-lying areas there are rich fertile soils, especially in eastern England. The mild climate and rainfall distributed over the whole year provide a long growing season; there is hardly ever a shortage of water, and grassland is green throughout the year.

The following table will tell you the changes in **livestock** from 1975–1985. The figures are in millions, so 14.7 stands for 14,700,000!

	1975	1983	1984	1985
Cattle and calves	14.7	13.3	13.2	12.8
Sheep and lambs	28.4	34.1	34.8	35.6
Pigs	8.0	8.2	7.7	7.9
Poultry	140.1	127.6	127.5	128.9

Our next table will give you the figures for **main crops**. They stand for million tonnes.

	1975	1983	1984
Wheat	5.3	10.8	14.9
Barley	8.4	10.0	11.1
Oats	0.8	0.5	0.5
Potatoes	5.4	5.9	7.4
Oilseed (e.g. rape)	0.07	0.6	0.9
Sugar beet	5.5	7.5	9.1

Here are a few examples to show you how the production of tonnes per hectare has gone up in the past ten years: Wheat from 4.4 to 6.3, barley from 3.6 to 4.9, potatoes from 25.1 to 35.8, and oilseed from 2.0 to 3.0 tonnes per hectare.

(Adapted from: *Britain 1987. An official handbook.*)

Words

hectare /'hektɑ:/ – measure for the area of land which equals 10,000 square metres; many farmers in Britain still measure their land in *acres* /'eɪkəz/: an acre equals a little over 4,000 square metres; *under crop* – used by farmers to grow grain, fruit, or vegetables; *soil* – the top covering of the earth in which plants grow; *livestock* – animals kept on a farm; *cattle* – large four-legged animals such as cows kept on a farm; *poultry* /'pəʊltrɪ/ – farmyard birds such as hens, ducks, etc.; *rape* – (German: Raps).

Questions

7. The numbers of some farm animals have gone up in Britain, others have gone down in the past ten years. Can you offer an explanation? (Remember that Britain joined the EEC in 1973!)
8. The production per hectare has gone up for most crops during the past couple of years. What may be the reasons?

Contents of the documentary film, part B

It took Linda a short ride only to get from Whitby across the North Yorkshire Moors into one of the most fertile parts of England, North Yorkshire. It is here that she comes across two different ways of farming.

Her first visit is to Norman Stockdale's farm, which is fairly small. We see Norman giving his two sheepdogs some practice in working with sheep. Obviously, the younger one still has to learn not to be afraid of the sheep. One of the harder jobs in raising sheep is the dipping: the sheep have to be dipped into water with chemicals in it to kill bugs and other pests in their fleece, and the sheep do not like that dipping at all.

Linda joins Norman and his wife in a stable and helps to bottle-feed lambs which are too weak to survive in the open. She then asks Norman a couple of questions. Since his answers are not easy to understand because of his Yorkshire accent, we will print out the conversation for you:

Linda:		Norman, you told me you came here in 1931. Now, that's 55 years ago.
Norman:		Yes, yes.
Linda:		How have things changed since then?
Norman:		Well, unbelievable really. You can't sort of compare when I was a little lad then to what things are like now. Which you know everything then was done by hand and now we have every mechanical device you can think of nearly. Costs a fortune, but that's what things are like now.
Linda:		So was it for the better?
Norman:		I would think 90%, yes. Ah, ... I wouldn't ..., there is only certain things I would like to go back, but the majority I prefer what we get of now.
Linda:		I'd love to see some of the farm.
Norman:		Aye?
Linda:		Yes.
Norman:		Yeah.

(When Norman was not on camera, he gave Linda an example for "certain things I would like to go back", and that were the many trees and the hedges between the fields which made a good home for birds and small animals.)

When Norman takes Linda round the farm she can tell by the barns and agricultural machines that Norman also grows crops. In other words, he does mixed farming, like most farmers did in the past. Finally they get to a duck pond. Norman explains:

> "There are not so many ponds left now on the farms. A lot of them have been drained and, you know, qualified for grants into the bargain.
> And, I thought, well, I'd like to keep mine, and so I applied for a grant to clean it out. And I wanted to put a fence round it, and plant some nice trees, willows and that sort of thing. But..., this anyway, this is as far as I've got with it. I've never got the fence up yet."

Next Linda visits John Marsay's farm. It is only a couple of miles from Norman's. Linda can see at once that John's is a completely different type of farm. It looks rather like a modern factory. When John took over from his father, he decided to give up mixed farming and to concentrate on a few crops only, like potatoes and oilseed. In one of the huge barns Linda says to John:

Linda:		You must be able to store hundreds of tonnes of potatoes here.
John:		Yes, in this store we can store 2..., over 2000 tonnes.
Linda:		And how long can you keep them for?
John:		Well, we can keep them from October right away through till end of June, beginning of July.

Linda:		And how do you keep them fresh?
John:		Well, we keep them fresh by blowing air through tunnels, which is no problem.
Linda:		And when do you let them go?
John:		Well, depending on the price… You know, if the prices were good over Christmas time, we would sell quite a few over Christmas. If they weren't, we'd keep them till later.
Linda:		So you wait till the price is right?
John:		Yes, that's correct. Yes.
Linda:		Has Britain's joining the EEC had much of an effect on farming life?
John:		It has. It's helped us to equip up for the potato market and put a better sample on to the housewife's table.
Linda:		Mm…, but on the farmer as such?
John:		Yes it's…, we've been able to build all these new buildings and buy new machinery. I think we'd have been able to do this in any case, even if we hadn't had the grants, but we're doing it in a shorter time.

The last thing we see on John's farm is a huge potato harvester that does the work which, in the past, would have kept a large number of farmhands busy.

Words

fleece /fli:s/ – a sheep's woollen coat; *lad* – boy, young man; *aye* – yes; *drain* – cause to become dry or empty; *qualify for grants* – fulfil all the conditions necessary to obtain money from the government (here: EEC money); *into the bargain* /ˈbɑːgɪn/ – in addition; *apply for* – here: ask for (a grant) by writing (to the government); *equip* /ɪˈkwɪp/ – get oneself all that is necessary for doing something.

Questions

9. What are the main differences between Norman Stockdale's and John Marsay's farms?
10. Why does John store his potatoes instead of selling them all at once after harvesting?

*Agricultural policies

The British Government aims to help the agriculture industry to grow and to become more and more efficient. This is done by providing research, advisory services and financial support, through measures to control disease, pests and pollution, and a better marketing for food and food products. The Government also encourages the farmers to aim for high standards on animal welfare. There are plans to give agriculture ministers a responsibility to achieve a balance between the interests of rural areas, conservation of nature, and recreation.

The Government is keen to encourage the growth of exports. In 1985 exports of food and drink amounted to £ 4,728 million, with the main markets being Western Europe, North America and the Middle East. Exports include speciality products such as fresh salmon, Scotch whisky, biscuits, jams and conserves, as well as beef, lamb, and cheese.

The stated aims of the European Community's agricultural policy are to increase agricultural productivity and thereby to make sure that the agricultural community has a fair standard of living, and that regular supplies of food can be guaranteed at reasonable prices.

The British Government has sought to obtain improvements in the operation of the Community's agricultural policy in order to reduce its costs. In 1985-86 expenditures in Britain on price guarantees, grants and subsidies were estimated to be £320 million, and those on the Community's agricultural policy £1,890 million. About £1,310 million was reimbursed from the Community budget.

(Adapted from: *Britain 1987. An official handbook.*)

Words

advisory /əd'vaɪzərɪ/ *services* – services to help (farmers) to come to good decisions (what to grow where and when); *support* (n) – help; *rural* – concerning country and village life; *amount to* – be equal to; *increase* /ɪn'kriːs/ (v) – make larger; *agricultural community* – the farmers and their families and farmhands; *expenditure* /ɪk'spendɪtʃə/ – spending; *subsidy* /'sʌbsədɪ/ – money paid by the government to make prices lower; *reimburse* /ˌriːɪm'bɜːs/ – pay back.

C

Focus on language: Auxiliary verbs

Auxiliary means "offering or giving help". Auxiliary verbs offer help to express ourselves in many ways. The ones we use most are the **primary auxiliaries** *be, have, do*. They help us to form the compound tenses, to form questions, or to express a negation:

> I **am** reading. – We **have** met many people. – He **was** surprised. – What **did** you see? – She **does not** believe him.

Let us have a closer look at the auxiliary *do*! Joe Green used it a lot when he met Linda at the top of the 199 steps:

> (1) You did it! – (2) How do you like our wonderful British summer? – (3) Why don't we go this way...? – (4) What do you do when you're not doing research in Britain? – (5) What's an American doing teaching English to Germans in Germany?

These sentences demonstrate three different ways in which *do* can be used: a) as a regular verb *(She does her work very well.)*; b) to form a question; c) as an "empty" verb which does not carry any real meaning but just stresses an action *(You do make a lot of mistakes!).*

Here are some more examples of the use of *do*:

119

(6) He did go to the office yesterday. – (7) What are you doing here? – (8) Does she have to write all those letters? – (9) He didn't steal the car, did he? – (10) How do you do? – (11) You do know how to run a farm!

Besides the primary auxiliaries there are a number of **modal auxiliaries:** *will/would, can/could, shall/should, may/might, must, need.* They help to express different modes or aspects of an action, e.g.:

She **will** help you = she is prepared or willing to help;
   or: she will do it at some point in the future.
She **can** help you = she has got the time or is able to do so.
She **must** help you = she is forced or feels the moral obligation to do so.

Let us have a closer look at the modal auxiliary *would*. The examples are once again taken from the interviews which you have heard and seen in the documentary films of this unit:

(12) The Pope at that time wouldn't allow the divorce. – (13) You come over here and pick up the stones (of the abbey). Wouldn't you do it? – (14) If there was one thing that I would notice it's the fishing boats. 25 years ago the harbour would have been full of herring boats. – (15) I would think (that farm life is a lot easier today). – (16) I'd love to see some of the farm. Would you show me around?

In these sentences, *would* is used to express a number of different modes or aspects: the condition under which an action takes place (or might take place); carefulness in what somebody says; politeness; expression of remembering what something was like in the past. In one instance *would* is used in the sense of "want to". The second of the following exercises will help you to see the different uses of the auxiliary *would* even more clearly.

Exercises
1. In which of the examples nos. (1) – (11) is *do* used as a regular verb, or to form a question, or to express a negation, or to stress an action?
      (1) regular verb – (2) ...

2. Translate examples (12) to (16) into German! (You will see that you will have to use different German expressions to show the different functions of *would*.) Try to note after each sentence which mode or aspect is expressed by the auxiliary *would*!

3. Give the following sentences a more polite form by using *would*!

Help me! – Show me the way to the castle! – I want to see your new potato harvester. – Can I borrow your bicycle? – She wants to hear more about the fishing industry.

4. Translate the conversation between Linda and Arthur Coulson (at the end of the contents of part A, pp.113–114). Do not translate word by word, but try to come up with a good German version of that conversation. After you have finished, make sure that your translation contains all the information given by Arthur Coulson!

Borders we have crossed
People we have met

Unit 39

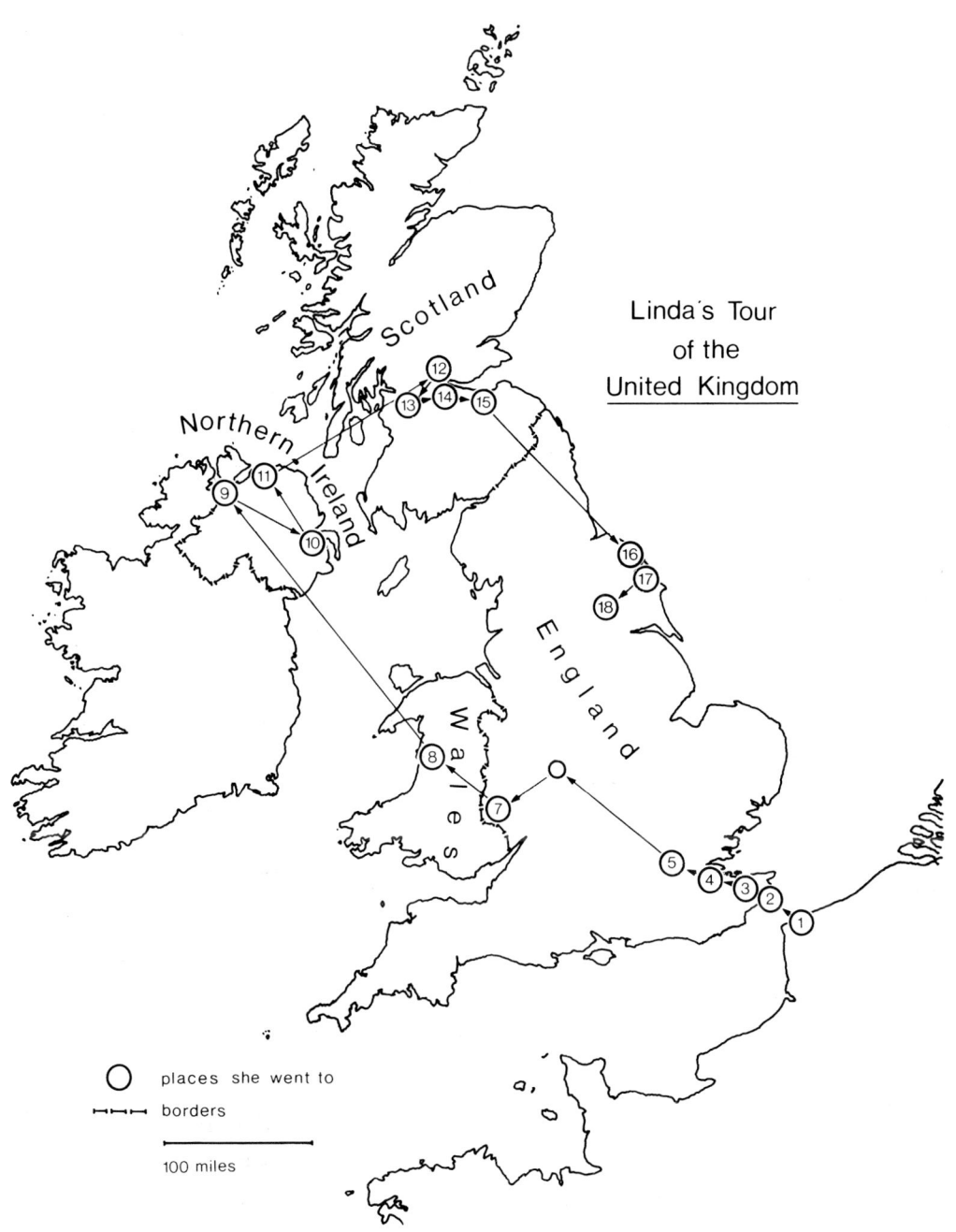

121

Looking back on Linda's tour of the United Kingdom

This last unit is different from the other twelve you have followed. Linda looks back on her tour through the four countries that form the United Kingdom. She remembers the borders she has crossed, the people she has met, and the places she has seen.
Since we have joined her on her journey, let us also join her in her retrospection – in her thoughts about the past weeks of travelling.

Question: What do you remember?

Try to trace back Linda's tour starting in Dover and ending in Yorkshire. List the places she visited and the people she met. Perhaps you can even remember some details, e.g. buildings she saw, or the subjects she talked about with the people.
The map on page 121 will help you. Follow the numbers on that map and start your list like this:

1. *Ferry to Dover. Captain Mike Western. Talks about the Channel Tunnel (=Chunnel).*

2. *Dover. Charles Willet, owner of a pub. He took Linda around Dover Castle. Talks about the history of the town.*

3. ...

A
Contents of the first part of the unit

Linda joins Paul in the studio. They talk about the **borders** Linda has crossed as she travelled from England to Wales, from Wales to Northern Ireland, from there to Scotland, and then back to England again.

But she has not only crossed the borders between these countries. She has crossed other types of borders as well, for instance **borders of time**, from Britain's past to Britain's present (e.g. in unit 27 A when she discussed the "Chunnel" problem with the captain and Dover's history with the pub owner). She has crossed **cultural borders** (e.g. in Birmingham with it's multi-racial society) and **language borders** as well (e.g. when, in Wales, she met a young lady who spoke a Celtic language)...

This idea of crossing borders or being on some kind of border is what the theme song of all 13 units of this course is about. You have heard parts of it again and again. In our first film today you will hear it one more time, and you will see some of the borders again which Linda has crossed. Jake Thackray, who wrote the words and the music, is from Yorkshire, but he has made the Border Country between England and Wales his home.

Borders

We stand here side by side.
We are so near and so divided.
We always draw this line.
How do we ever come together,
5 Me to your side, you to mine?

We feel these borders in the bones.
We draw these borders in the head,
And down the middle of the road,
Up the middle of the bed.
10 The north, the south; the left and the right;
The orange and green; the black and the white.
We build more walls than we build bridges.

We stand here side by side.
We are so near and so divided.
15 We always draw this line.
How do we ever come together,
Me to your side, you to mine?

We've got these borders in the blood;
Under the skin, deep in the heart.
20 We feel the need to keep together,
We keep the need to feel apart.
The here and the there, the now and the then,
The me and the you; the us, the them.
We live forever on the borders!

We stand here side by side...

(Words and music by Jake Thackray)

Most of Jake's songs are very difficult to understand, sometimes even for his fellow countrymen. But since he knew that this song was for a German audience, he did his best to avoid difficult words and phrases. So the lyrics of "Borders" do not need much explaining. "Orange and green" in line 11 refer to the Unionists and Republicans in Northern Ireland, of course "black and white" to multi-racial situations like the ones we have seen in Birmingham. Lines 20 and 21 refer to the mixed feelings we often have: on the one hand, we feel that it would be best for all of us not to fight each other, but, on the other, we stick to our old habits of seeing the differences between ourselves and our neighbours.

39

The only thing which will be new to you in the documentary film that goes with Jake Thackray's song is **Hadrian's Wall**. It is an "Ancient Monument", as we read on a table by the wall. It is at the same time a reminder that people have always drawn border lines. This wall, named after the Roman Emperor Hadrian (117–138 A.D.), was built by the Romans in the north of England to protect this part of their Empire against the Picts and Scots, who are among the forefathers of the Scottish people.

Question: What borders do you remember?

In our summary we have mentioned the different types of borders which Linda crossed on her tour. We have also given a few examples. Try to find some more!

B
Contents of the second part of the unit

Hadrian's Wall

Linda and Paul continue their talks about the journey. What does Linda remember about **the people she met**? What impressions has she written down in the diary which she kept while she was touring the U.K.?

She was impressed by the warmth and friendliness of the people. As in her own country, the USA, the British nearly always use *first names*, calling her Linda, and asking her to call them Charles or Sue or Emma – or whatever their first names were. That, of course, helps you to feel comfortable and to build up personal contacts.

At the same time Linda was struck by the *pride* of the British. She felt that they were always proud of their town, of the part of the country they lived in, and of the whole country. They made visitors from abroad feel welcome. On the other hand, many of them told her that they want to stay an island. "The Continent", as they call the rest of Europe, is just over 20 miles across the Channel, and they feel that is close enough.

Towards the end of their conversation Paul asks Linda: Would she, from her own experience, give the viewer a few *practical tips*?

Linda's first tip is on traffic. Everybody knows that in the U.K. people drive on the left. But still, when they cross a street, foreigners look first left, then right, as they are used to doing in their home countries. Linda's advice: never forget to look *first right, then left* in the U.K.!

Hotels she found are terribly expensive. Here her advice is to go for "B & B", for bed and breakfast places, where you can really feel at home.

The language was no problem for her as an American. She does not think that it will be a problem for visitors from other countries, either, because the British are very kind and will always help you out when they notice that you are not familiar with some of the words and phrases they use.

She and Paul then remember some of the people Linda met. We join them and meet again:

- Charles Willet and the people in his pub;
- Frances Kennedy, showing Linda round Belfast;
- Jerry Tyrrel of Holiday Projects West in Londonderry/Derry;
- Olwyn Lloyd Evans, the Welsh-speaking young lady from a bank in Dolgellau;
- Jake Thackray who sings yet another song – a silly one, as he says himself.

Linda's conversation with one of the customers in the pub is yet another example for the wish of many Britains to remain an island:

Linda:	And what about this Chunnel?
	Do you really think they're going to build it after all?
Neighbour:	Not if I can help it!
	Why do we need it? Can you give me a reason?
Charles Willet:	I think the lady's asking you if you have a reason.
Neighbour:	Well, fine. – We don't need the Tunnel.
	If anyone wants to get across to France by car, they don't have to have a tunnel through there, wasting money like that . . . .
	If they want to get to France in half an hour, they can do it in a car by Hovercraft.
Linda:	Well, it would bring you closer to the Continent!
Neighbour:	We're close enough now with 22 miles between us.
Customers in bar:	Hear, hear!
Neighbour:	We've never had a good working relationship with France. When we went into the EEC, we had problems. I don't

39

really see any need for a Channel tunnel whatsoever!

If you're talking about commercial traffic, lorries – which incidentally I'm connected with – they do not need to get to France in half an hour.

You're saving half-an-hour's travelling time at the cost of God knows how many millions...!

When Frances Kennedy and Linda drive past the docks in Belfast, we are reminded that there are problems everywhere in Northern Ireland:

Linda: Look at all those giant cranes.
Frances: Yes, they're the cranes which belong to the shipyard, Harland and Wolff.
It's an important place in Belfast, because it employed a lot of people.
But there's also been a lot of controversy about it, because at one stage there was a lot of unfairness.
They only employed Protestants at one stage. That was very..., there's a lot of prejudice there.
Things have changed a bit.
Linda: There isn't that much business going on?
Frances: Not a lot. Like shipbuilding everywhere.

But, despite these problems, Northern Ireland is the country which Linda liked most of all. And she is not the only one! Jerry Tyrrel, who came over from England, has decided to stay. This is what he told Linda:

"Derry is a great place to live. It's a great place to visit as well.
Sometimes people are a wee bit scared of coming to Northern Ireland, but usually, once they've been, they want to come back again.
I find this a lot.
Also people are very friendly. It's a bit of a cliché, but again it's something which everybody finds.
And they're very tolerant of the individual. A good way of describing it is that they give you enough rope to hang yourself or to skip!
So I enjoy living here. I never made a conscious decision to stay, but it would have to be something really special to take me away from it."

Words

working relationship – partnership; *controversy* /kənˈtrɒvəsɪ/ – argument about something over which there is much disagreement; *at one stage* – at a certain time; *prejudice* /ˈpredʒədɪs/ – unfair and unfavourable feeling not based on reason or enough knowledge; *wee* – Scottish and Northern Irish for "little"; *conscious decision* – a decision made after giving the matter much thought.

Question: Where would you like to go?

Following Linda on her tour of the United Kingdom, you have heard and seen quite a bit of the country – or, to be more correct, of the *four* countries. If you had a chance to go to the U.K., which part or parts would you choose for a longer stay? Try to give reasons for your decision!

C

Focus on language

In this final unit of our course there is no special subject from English grammar. Instead, Linda reminds you that grammar was not invented by teachers to make life hard for their students. It was the language which came first – the language as it is spoken by the people in order to inform one another and to tell each other their ideas, wishes and hopes. And that is why we have taken all the examples in our focus-on-language parts straight from the conversations Linda had with people in the U.K.

To this Paul added a good piece of advice to you all: **Don't be afraid to make mistakes**! Of course, if you don't open your mouth you will not make any mistakes. But you will not learn the language, either!

We hope that you do open your mouth and talk a lot with your TELEKOLLEG partners and teachers. And we hope that you listen to speakers of English and talk to them whenever there is a chance. There are a lot of English speaking people in this country – tourists, business people, soldiers…!

We also hope that these 13 units have helped you to take a big step forward in your knowledge of English. We wish you continuing success in your efforts to learn English!

39

Answers to questions. Solutions to exercises

Unit 27

Here are some suggestions on how to answer the **questions**.

1. Dover has always been an important town and port in British history because of its position on the coast of south-east England. This has made it one of the main gateways to Britain from Roman times to the present day.

2. In the past, of course, the fact that Britain was surrounded by the sea made it very difficult for the island to be invaded. However, nowadays, as a member of the EEC, this is surely no longer important: the U.K. is now part of the European Community and must do everything not to separate itself from the Continent, but to draw closer and closer to it.

3. (Here, of course, we cannot give an answer for you. You should weigh up the facts given in the introduction and decide for yourself.)

4. On the car ferry, the car-drivers have time for a rest. They can stretch their legs a bit and perhaps have a meal as well. Psychologically, the ferry gives them time to adjust themselves mentally to the idea of driving on the other side of the road when they land.
   Another big advantage is that you can go on deck and enjoy some fresh air, whereas in a tunnel you just have to sit and wait until you have passed right through it. A lot of people will be worried about being underground for such a relatively long time.
   Many people also enjoy the opportunity to do some duty-free shopping on the ferry.

5. Here are some of the main differences:
   a) You cannot get a drink at any time of the day or in the early hours of the morning because the opening and closing times are laid down by law. Pubs are generally open from about 10.30 a.m. to 3 p.m. and again from about 5.30 p.m. to 10.30 or 11.00 in the evening. However, this will soon be changed so that you can get a drink from 11 a.m. to 11 p.m.
   b) Children under 14 are not allowed to go into places where alcohol is served.
   c) You have to be 18 or over to buy or drink alcohol in a pub.
   d) There are a number of bars in a pub, e.g. the public bar, the saloon bar.
   e) You have to go up to the bar and order your drink yourself. And you pay for it immediately.

6. First of all, oil and gas have become much cheaper, whereas it is expensive to mine coal. Secondly, nuclear energy was seen as a more economical and reliable way of producing electricity (but see unit 32). Thirdly, there was strong competition from countries where labour costs (= what you have to pay the workers in the mines) were much lower, so that is was often cheaper to import coal.

7. There are fewer opportunities for a man like Norman Dans in Wales because the coal industry there has gone through very difficult times indeed and a lot of the mines there have been closed down. The unemployment in the coal-mining areas of South Wales is very high.

Exercises

1. a) – I'd like to go to the Castle.
      – Soon as we close, my dear, I'll take you.
      – I'd love to go there. Would you really?
      – Yes, certainly.

   b) – Do you know I'm a Dovorian myself. Dover, Vermont.
        Ever heard of the place?
      – I have. I think you've got two or three Dovers in America, haven't you? Not as good as this one.

   c) – So you're not from Dover?
      – No... Well, I'm from Kent but not from Dover. I've lived in Dover a long time.
      – Too long, if you ask me.

d) – Well, it's kept people out for a long time, hasn't it?
   – It certainly has.

2. a) fortify   b) successor   c) a car ferry   d) look after   e) look for   f) an orchard   g) commute   h) go through a bad patch

3. Die Grafschaft Kent ist beispielsweise als der Garten Englands bekannt. Da der Boden gut, das Klima mild, die Niederschläge regelmäßig, aber mäßig waren, haben dort die Römer Obstgärten und Weinberge angelegt, und bis zum heutigen Tag ist Kent für sein Obst, vor allem für Äpfel und Birnen, Pflaumen, Kirschen und Erdbeeren bekannt.
Typisch für die Landschaft Kents sind die grünen Wiesen, die vielen Bäume und Hecken, die Schaf- und Rinderherden und schließlich die schönen alten strohgedeckten Häuser. Das Straßennetz ist so gut, daß viele, die in Kent wohnen, jeden Tag zwischen ihrem Zuhause und London pendeln.

Unit 28

Here are some suggestions on how to answer the **questions**.

1. A lot of people live and work in London, so there would be many deaths. The economic life of the capital would be completely disrupted. Flooding would pollute the water supplies in London. As a final example, the London underground, one of the fastest means of travel, would be out of action for about a year.

2. The new ships built in recent years are all very large and so they require water deeper than the Thames. However, the main reason is almost certainly the specialization that has gone hand in hand with the bigger ships. Cargo is handled differently now: most goods are transported in containers. The loading and unloading of containers require different port facilities. Most of the containers in the London area are now no longer handled in London but further down the Thames estuary, where Tilbury has become the main container port.

3. Well, you see a lot of wharfs and warehouses being pulled down or converted into office buildings and flats. Again there are not a lot of ships transporting goods to be seen on the Thames nowadays.

4. Here are some of the main advantages: firstly, the City is very small, so that everything is concentrated within a very small area; secondly, its geographical position places it roughly half way between the financial markets in the Far East and in the USA; thirdly, the language used in the City is also the language of international business, English; and, finally, the City has been a commercial trading centre for centuries, so that a lot of knowhow and experience have been collected there.

5. The City will have to adapt to the changing needs of the modern business world. For instance, modern communications technology (e.g. the computer; telex and telefax machines) means that there is really no need for insurance to be concentrated in just one building or stocks and shares to be sold in yet another building. The city will have to make sure that it is far more internationally minded than its competitors if it wants to remain one of the great financial centres of the world.

6. There is a long tradition of doing business in London. The town started as a Roman trading-post and trade has since then continued to dominate life there. The City of London keeps alive the international tradition; the street markets keep the traditions alive within the various local communities in London. In a very real sense then, the London markets are the lifeblood of the metropolis.

7. Both markets and pubs help to keep old traditions alive and encourage in the local people the feeling of belonging to a community or, to put it differently, they encourage the "community spirit".

Exercises

1. a) caused   b) have caused   c) inaugurated   d) devastated   e) has managed   f) have disappeared, have sprung up   g) originated   h) enabled

2. a) for   b) since   c) for   d) since   e) since   f) for   g) since   h) since

3. Ohne die Themse hätte sich London niemals zu der wichtigen Stadt entwickeln können, die sie tatsächlich geworden ist. Man sollte nie vergessen, daß der Hauptgrund, weswegen eine Stadt hier in erster Linie

entstand, war, daß es an dieser Stelle der Themse möglich war, sowohl eine Brücke als auch einen Hafen zu bauen. Durch die Brücke wurden die Entfernungen auf dem Landweg kürzer, und das bedeutete, daß London mit der Zeit unvermeidlich zum Mittelpunkt eines ausgedehnten Straßennetzes wurde; durch den Hafen verbesserten sich die Verbindungen zu den Ländern jenseits des Kanals und den Schiffen wurde es ermöglicht, mit den Gezeiten ein- und auszufahren.

Unit 29

Here are some suggestions on how to answer the **questions.**

1. Dailies and evening papers come out every day of the week. They can be divided into "quality" papers and "popular" papers or "tabloids". A quality paper in West Germany would be the *Süddeutsche Zeitung* (Munich), whereas the *Bild* (Berlin) would be considered a tabloid. A well-known German weekly is *Die Zeit* (Hamburg), and *Der Spiegel* (Hamburg) would be a political magazine.

2. The introduction of computers in the newspaper industry has meant different things for different people. For many printers it has meant unemployment because their craft is no longer needed. Journalists have to get used to writing on computers rather than on typewriters. However, they will see their articles in print sooner. For most newspaper owners computers mean more profit because they seem more efficient and less expensive than people.

3. Popular papers and quality papers differ in their format: qualities are larger. The use of headlines and pictures is different too. But they are also considered to differ in quality and their readerships. Populars focus on sensations more than on information, and qualities address themselves to more educated and more powerful readers.

4. The newsvendor points out the different groups of qualities and populars and is well aware of which paper belongs to which group. The editor also discusses the range of topics covered in a paper and the freedom of journalists to write according to their conscience only. "Honest reporting" and "a broad sense of politics" seem to make for the quality of a good newspaper.

5. The parties mentioned are the Tories or Conservatives, the Labour Party, and the Alliance, a new group of Social Democrats and Liberals. The only British paper supporting Labour seems to have been the *Daily Mirror. The Guardian* opposed the Conservatives also, but for different reasons. In elections the Labour Party finds practically no support in the press because newspaper owners tend to be conservative rather than socialist.

6. Free papers are weekly newspapers published in all parts of the U.K. and distributed free. They are paid by commercial firms rather than by the readers. Therefore most of their space will be devoted to advertisements. Their main purpose seems to be to inform consumers about products and goods sold in their town. In West Germany, too, so-called *Anzeigenblätter* are also distributed free to each household.

7. In participant sports people are involved actively whereas in spectator sports they only watch the event. It is not easy to draw the line between both kinds of sports. But it would be safe to say that football – both in the U.K. and the FRG – attracts more spectators than active participants. Jogging and running, on the other hand, seem to involve many people actively and would therefore be a good example of participant sports.

8. Cricket is becoming more popular in the U.K. It is played by many people in many towns, and many amateur clubs exist. Golf, on the other hand, still seems limited to better-off club members. Cricket also draws more spectators than golf and is played by teams.

9. The writer of the leader is worried that racism may be dangerous to cricket. He seems to think that black and white people – both players and spectators – used to get along well in cricket. Racial conflicts would then hurt the peaceful competition in such matches.

10. The letter to the editor disagrees with the leader. But after reading the opening sentence, the reader gets the impression that there is actually less racial abuse in cricket. However, what the writer is actually trying to say is that racial abuse in cricket is not new, but has been there for a long time.

Exercises

1. a) and/who/and/whilst/that/what/when
   b) who own us ...   : relative clause
      whilst I'm editor ...   : concessional clause
      that the tradition ...   : nominal clause
      what the proprietor says ...   : relative clause
      when he picks up the phone ... : temporal clause

   c) <u>We</u> do very much believe and the people who own us – and I'm one of them whilst I'm editor – <u>believe</u> ...

2. When (a) in 1975 ...,
   (l) public interest ...

   Although (b) its use ...,
   (g) about half of ...

   (c) No Commonwealth countries ...
   because (h) its government ...

   (d) Today ...
   which (i) is published ...

   (e) More than 70 ...
   (j) 40 of which are ...

   Although (f) this ...,
   (k) national newspapers ...

3. Wir sollten doch diesen Mythos endlich aufgeben, daß Cricket von solchen Störungen relativ frei ist. Viele Leute sind auf Cricketplätzen deshalb rassistisch, weil viele auch außerhalb rassistisch sind. Das sichere Gefühl, sich als Zuschauer in einer größeren Menge verstecken zu können, gibt ihnen eine ausgezeichnete Gelegenheit zur Äußerung ihrer häßlichen Ansichten. Als Gegner des Rassismus habe ich mich bei solchen Situationen niemals in der Mehrheit befunden.

Unit 30

Here are some suggestions on how to answer the **questions**.

1. Public schools in the U.K. are not state schools, but private institutions with tuition fees. These schools have a long tradition and a high prestige for educating the elite. Comprehensive schools are run by the state educational authorities and have been set up in practically all towns. These schools take all pupils from a given district regardless of money and intelligence.

2. There are practically no German schools which could be compared to British public schools. However, a small number of private boarding schools might be somewhat similar. There are comprehensive schools in West Germany, and they are called *Gesamtschulen*. In contrast to the situation in England and Wales, comprehensives have not replaced the traditional secondary school types, but are usually offered in addition to them.

3. They were not filmed on school grounds or within classes, but only outside and without teachers. They seem very self-confident and well-educated; they come from all parts of the world and include girls as well. They did not tell a lot about their real school life as such.

4. Holland Park Comprehensive seems to be a modern and progressive school. Pupils wear no school uniforms and are expected to behave like young adults rather than as children. This is true for their discipline and for their learning. Perhaps a woman as the head of the school makes a difference too.

5. State money is, of course, necessary for keeping the buildings in good condition and for paying teachers' salaries. In recent years expenses for the state school system have been cut. On the other hand, private schools seem to have enough money and can therefore offer a better education for the children of the rich.

6. The school system in the U.K. can be considered elitist for various reasons. A number of independent schools offer an expensive education which only rich parents can afford. The majority of children have to go to state schools. Many of these pupils leave school at 16, and only some of them go on to universities.

7. The boy must be black and was apparently not able to read at the age of nine. He was therefore put into special classes for slow learners. His language is partly non-standard and shows traces of black English, e.g. "man", "cool". At the same time his descriptions of people and situations are very vivid and show some humour too.

8. His basic experience at school was that white teachers cannot avoid discriminating against black children. He thinks that his white teacher behaves unconsciously in this way because she has been educated this way all her life. The black boy recognizes that discrimination will only be felt by those who are discriminated against.

9. Tertiary education follows secondary education and refers to universities mainly. People take part in further education when they have a job and want a better qualification in their profession. If only adults are concerned, one would speak of adult education which may include any kind of courses for both professional purposes and for leisure.

10. The Open University is open in many ways. It does not require a formal school-leaving certificate like other universities do. You do not have to attend a university, but can do your studies at home. Age or social status of OU students makes no difference.

11. Quite often you have to do your regular job and study in your spare time. You may have to watch TV courses early in the morning or over the weekend. Sometimes friends or family members may not understand what you are doing and why you are spending so much time for studying.

12. Joe seems to have more time for his studies after he lost his job. He has less problems generally than Cathie. In evaluating his experience at the OU Joe stresses the intellectual profits. Cathie seems more concerned about the good and bad social effects.

13. Studying at home is bound to put strains on family life. If your family is patient enough or shows some interest in your work, studying will be a lot easier. Sometimes families will have to do without you which may cause problems. On the other hand, family members will profit from new ideas and new outlooks on life.

Exercises

1. Joe said that studying at the OU had opened a new range on life. It broadened his concepts and ideas and made him question situations and facts that he would have allowed to pass unnoticed before. It made him think a little …, it made him use his brains a bit more. According to Joe it was also more important than one thought to talk over doing the course with members of one's family because they were going to be affected most.
Cathie thought that studying had increased her confidence a lot, that she could argue ideas better with other people and that that had been good. She also thought that it was sometimes difficult because friends did not understand what you were doing so you couldn't talk about it to them. If one had got a good tutorial group, it would help.

2. a) are/live/study
   b) come/range
   c) have included
   d) do not come together/are sent/are transmitted/is given
   e) concentrates/has been
   f) are used/are sold
   g) recommend

3. Es ist deshalb kein Wunder, daß englische Kinder in Rekordzahlen zu Privatschulen geströmt sind. Aber die Zahl der Plätze ist sehr beschränkt. (Gegenwärtig gibt es ungefähr 500 000 Schüler in den 2000 Privatschulen des Landes und 7 000 000 in den öffentlichen Schulen.) Kritiker behaupten, daß eine solche Entwicklung die verborgenen Klassenunterschiede verstärkt, die, wie sie es sehen, ohnehin die Ursache für das Problem sind. „Ich glaube nicht, daß die Engländer jemals Bildung besonders hoch geachtet haben", sagt Dr. John Rae, ehemaliger Leiter von Westminster, einer hoch angesehenen Privatschule. „Sie schicken einfach die

meisten Kinder auf die Straße, wenn sie 16 sind und lassen nur die allerklügsten zur Universität gehen. Wir sind sehr elitär eingestellt." Tatsächlich gehen nur etwa 30% aller Schüler aus staatlichen Schulen später an die Hochschule.

Unit 31

Here are some suggestions on how to answer the **questions**.

1. Raw materials must be shipped to the centres of production, e.g. iron ore and coal. Canals are very suitable for transporting such heavy goods. On the other hand, the finished industrial products have to be moved from the factories to other factories or to the customers.
2. Canals used to be the main means of transport. They connected inland factories with each other and with the seaports. The introduction of railways made shipping goods a lot faster. Today, transport by road has become a serious rival to railways. Even air freight is used more and more.
3. The song starts out like a love song, in a rather melancholy mood. As the setting changes from the dirtier parts of the town to clouds and cats, the song becomes perhaps more optimistic. Then memories of sight and sound come in, and the writer is still thinking about his love. The final verse comes as a shock. The girl seems totally forgotten and some unexplained aggressive mood has taken possession of the man.
4. Children used to work in every industry and might even be treated just like adult men. But often children would be employed in the so-called light industries which required less physical power, but more skilful hands. Sometimes children would work at home along with their mothers. In any case children could only earn pennies even though working hours were long and the competition was strong.
5. His opening sentence shows the author's sympathy "for the sheer misery" of people under such conditions. He tries to observe and report objectively and provide many details. Yet, some of the adjectives used tell us about his anger: laborious, squalid homes, hard work for little hands, terrible competition.
6. Riots start in different ways, e.g. after conflicts with the police. But the underlying reasons for unrest are social and cannot be found in either police intervention or in skin colour. The anger and frustration that surface in riots are caused by discrimination in housing, education, and on the job. Quite often unemployed young people will be involved, and second generation immigrants seem to feel discrimination more than others.
7. When a riot breaks out, the police will usually be called by one of the groups involved. Often the police will find themselves protecting the better off and well-to-do citizens and their property. Sometimes the mere presence of a police car may actually increase the tension. Therefore the police have been asked by civil rights groups to avoid confrontations and act behind the scenes, if possible.
8. The intercultural conflicts mentioned in the film do not appear very serious. We witness a telephone call complaining about the Muezzin's call for prayer. The police-officer talks about Sikh people carrying daggers in public and is also worried about punishment in mosque schools. Finally, the unequal distribution of black and white officers in the police forces is mentioned. The police themselves will have to change this.
9. Spoken language comes out well when the narrator tries to present dialogues and quote from bits of spoken speech, e.g. "asked me had he been … and did he have …", or "he kept saying no it was …". Also some sentences contain too many events, perhaps because of the speaker's excitement, e.g. "Anyway, the next morning … he stole it". The narrator also appears in person commenting and adding her own experience, e.g. "I mean, I have been …".
10. The girl is very bitter and resentful about the behaviour of the police. Her boyfriend, other people, and she, too, have been stopped by the police for no obvious reason. She seems to think that the police just want to show their power and make young and coloured people feel under observation.

Exercises

1. a) commit oneself to
   set up a committee
   look at issues
   concern (oneself) with

     b) links between the Council and groups
        groups within the city
        equality of opportunity for ... people
        issues in the areas
        links with the community
        appointments to the Unit
 2. a) up/in/of/in
    b) Behind/in/of/by
    c) in/to/in
    d) of/with/as/between/of
    e) in/with
    f) about
    g) to
    h) for/of/with
    i) to/to/in
 3. Jedenfalls, am nächsten Morgen habe ich ihn gesehen, und sein ganzes Gesicht war voller Quetschungen, und er hatte blaue Flecken an seinem ganzen Körper. Anscheinend hatten sie ihn geschlagen, weil sie ihm nicht glaubten, daß der Rasierer ein Geburtstagsgeschenk war; sie bestanden darauf, daß er ihn vielleicht gestohlen hätte. Als er weiterhin sagte, nein, es sei ein Geburtstagsgeschenk, schlugen sie ihn weiter. Solche Dinge legen den Schluß nahe, daß die Polizei rassistisch ist. Ich komme an Leuten vorbei, wenn sie von der Polizei angehalten werden. Ich meine, ich bin selbst schon in einem Auto gewesen, und die Polizei hat uns ohne jeglichen Grund angehalten, und sie wollten alle möglichen unwichtigen Informationen wissen, wie z.B., wer die anderen Leute im Auto außer dem Fahrer sind, und wohin wir fahren.

Unit 32

Here are some suggestions on how to answer the **questions**.

1. Nuclear energy has for a long time seemed to be safer and cleaner than other energy sources like coal. Also, uranium was said to be unlimited in contrast to both coal and oil. Since water is needed for cooling the system, most nuclear power stations are built either along the coast or on river banks.
2. There have always been groups of people who have warned about using nuclear energy in weapons and in power stations. But only in recent years has the public become more aware of the real risks involved. The first problem was how to get rid of nuclear waste that goes on radiating for centuries. And accidents in power stations like Harrisburg or Chernobyl have caused many people to doubt the security of nuclear power.
3. For one thing, he is worried about a big blow-up. In the special case of Berkeley Power Station the tide in the river would very quickly pollute the entire region. But he is also worried about the normal amount of radiation when the power station works under normal conditions.
4. The initiative was started by people who were worried about cancer in their region that may have been caused by nuclear radiation. They wanted better information about such risks to their health. Now they have decided that they need better protection against such dangers if they exist.
5. The article mentions nuclear military plants, nuclear research establishments, and nuclear power stations. It is alarming that not only nuclear power stations seem to radiate and possibly damage people's health.
6. The main finding is that children under 14 and adults seem to have a greater chance of suffering from cancer if they live close to nuclear power stations. But the researchers are not certain that the diseases observed are actually caused by nuclear radiation.
7. "Great Britain" is a geographical term and stands for England, Wales, and Scotland. The "United Kingdom" is more of a political term and includes Northern Ireland. "Britain" is sometimes used instead of "Great Britain". The "British Isles" include Britain and the whole of Ireland.
8. There are many unusual things in this area. It has for many centuries been the historical borderline between England and Wales and is still like a no-man's-land. The boundary itself is hard to find. In the Forest of Dean many strange traditions have survived both for the inhabitants and for their sheep.

9. There is no clear, regular metre. Some stanzas are too short, others too long. Some end-rhymes can be found, but there is no regular rhyming pattern. However, quite often words close together sound quite similar. They either start with the same consonant or have similar vowel sounds, e.g. "bane of his life – bitch of a wife", "howl and scowl", "shudder and shake". These alliterations and semi-rhymes come out well in singing.

10. The audience seems to really enjoy this song. For non-native people the humour is not always easy to understand. But it seems to rely mostly on clichés about men and women and quarrels between them. The song-writer – as a man – has decided to have the man win over the woman. Is that perhaps why people find it so funny?

Exercises

1. a) If/were built/could produce
   b) If/want to see/(will) have to travel
   c) If/is built/will fill
   d) When/returns/is channeled/generates
   e) If/are designed/will have
   f) If/is/can be subdivided
   g) If/is/are required
   h) When/is built/brings
   i) If/compare/can be built
   j) When/decided to stop/ended

2. Nun, anfangs war es unser Ziel, daß es eine öffentliche Untersuchung geben müsse über diese Vorfälle von Krebs bei Kindern und über die Möglichkeit einer Verbindung zwischen diesen Fällen und den Emissionen von Kraftwerken. Wir meinen auch, daß es hinsichtlich der Strahlungsmengen viel intensivere Kontrollen geben muß. Außerdem glauben wir, daß unsere Gesundheit nicht hinreichend überwacht wird, wenn man an die Gefahr in dieser Region denkt, nämlich die Atomkraftwerke. Die Gesundheit der Menschen muß viel sorgfältiger beobachtet werden, so daß man tatsächlich weiß, was mit einem geschieht und ob eine Gefahr von diesen Einrichtungen ausgeht, von denen man uns sagt, daß sie völlig sicher seien.

3. Young parents could be most likely to agree with the message of this slogan. Especially after Chernobyl, families with young children in many parts of Europe were very much concerned about milk, food, and playgrounds. The slogan is critical of a traditional Western attitude towards nature and the earth. If you inherit something, you own it and can do with it as you please. However, nature can be damaged or even destroyed this way. Already many animals and plants have disappeared from the earth. Our environment is hostile to many living creatures. Some technologies and, of course, many weapons are a menace to the survival of mankind. At this point environmentalists ask for a new attitude to life and nature. Not exploiting the earth, but conserving it for future generations must be our aim. If we fail to understand this, our children may not be able to live.

Unit 33

Here are some suggestions on how to answer the **questions**.

1. Cardiff is no longer the "coal capital" of the world. Coal mines have been closed down in Wales as well as in Germany, the USA and in many other countries because coal is no longer much in demand. It has been largely replaced by oil, gas, and electricity from nuclear power plants. It is not much needed in the steel industry either since the demand for steel has gone down, too. So many Welsh miners have lost their jobs or have moved to places where they can still find work – like the Welsh miner whom Linda met in Kent (see unit 27 B!).

2. (We cannot suggest a general answer to this rather personal question. We can only ask now: Did you expect more, or fewer, or different things than you have seen at the centre?)

3. a) methods to *save* energy: better insulation of houses (thicker walls, quadruple glazing = four layers of glass in the windows), ovens and cookers …
   b) methods to *gain* energy from renewable sources: using solar power (solar walls, panels, and cells), wind power (windmills, wind turbines), water power (water wheels, water turbines) …

4. The use of alternative technology on a large scale basis would mean that fewer power plants burning coal, oil or gas would be needed. So there would be less pollution of the air. The resources of coal, oil and gas would last longer, too. We could even do without nuclear power stations and thus avoid the danger of radiations. Of course, many workers in the power plants would lose their jobs, but there would be new jobs in the production of turbines, solar panels etc. and in the construction of houses with better insulation.
   However, you can only make good use of sun power where there is enough sunshine, and wind power where the winds are strong enough and blow for long periods of time. And how can you use water power in places where rainfall is much less frequent than in Wales? It looks like a lot more research has to be done before these problems are solved.

5. Organic fertilizers used instead of chemicals: weeds and kitchen waste turned into compost; dung from animals, urine ("pee") …

6. It seems hard on the children to have to learn two languages. But most children are quick learners if they have the chance to hear both languages spoken a lot. And that is the case in Wales with some 600,000 speakers of Welsh.
   Of course, it means extra work to have all street, road and shop signs and all bills and other pieces of information made out in two languages. On the other hand, would it not be a shame to let a beautiful language die – a language which lends itself to story-telling and singing? And the Welsh people are great story-tellers and singers.

7. It is easier for the government and administration if they have to deal with the citizens in one language only. The main reason for the English trying to suppress the Welsh language, however, was their fear that the Welsh might try to separate from England and form a nation of their own – with their own language – which Wales had been up to the 15th century.

8. Beside the Celtic minority languages in Scotland, Ireland, and Brittany (France) there are many more countries with more than one language – e.g. Switzerland, Belgium, Cyprus, and Canada. One typical example for a minority language is the Maori language in New Zealand. It was declining rapidly after the British had begun to settle there some 200 years ago and had taken over the rule of the country. Now the Maoris try hard to revive their own language. They have started "language nests" in which Maori pre-school children learn the language of their forefathers.

Exercises

1. central, natural, national, practical, physical, mathematical, geographical, logical.

2. organ   – organic (adj.), organize (v), organism (n), organization (n)
   develop – development (n), developmental (adj.), developing (e.g. in "developing country"), developer (noun meaning a chemical substance used to develop films)
   nation   – national (adj.), nationalism (n), nationality (n), nationalist (n), nationalistic (adj.), international (adj.), nationalize (verb meaning the action of a government to gain the control of a business or an industry) …

3. act   – actor, action
   produce   – producer, production
   invent   – inventor, invention
   inspect   – inspector, inspection
   insulate – insulator (an object or material which insulates), insulation
   Note, that in some cases the pronunciation changes, e.g. /prəˈdjuːs/ but /prəˈdʌkʃn/!

4. Here are the German technical terms corresponding to the English ones Tim Brown used:
   Energie, Elektrizität, Turbinen, Reservoir, Effekte, Pestizide, Agrikultur, organisch, System, Zyklus, praktizieren, nuklear, Alternativen, Technologien, Projekte.

5. Den größten Teil unserer Energie erhalten (gewinnen) wir aus Energiequellen, die sich nicht erschöpfen (wörtlich: aus erneuerbaren Energiequellen). Die erste (Quelle) ist Sonnen-Kraft. Wir haben (hier) Solar-Kollektoren, die uns mit einer gewissen Menge von Heißwasser versorgen, vor allem im Sommer, und mit Elektrizität. Wir haben auch eine ziemliche Anzahl von Windturbinen, Windmühlen, die Elektrizität für die Beleuchtung und für einen Großteil der Warmwasserbereitung produzieren. Und in unseren Bergen haben wir ein Reservoir (Staubecken), das mit Wasser gefüllt ist; das treibt zwei Wasserturbinen. Sie liefern für

unser Zentrum etwa vier Kilowatt Strom. Das (= die Wasserkraft) ist in Wales wirklich die verläßlichste Energiequelle, denn hier regnet es immer. Das Reservoir ist also ständig voll.

Unit 34

Here are some suggestions on how to answer the **questions**.

1. The Troubles in Northern Ireland are certainly not just a religious problem. They originate in the constant attempts by England to dominate the whole of Ireland. One of the means adopted by the English kings was the policy of "Plantation". Thus a great injustice was done to the original inhabitants of Ulster. This meant that the historical problem also became a social problem. We can add to these considerations the fact that the Protestants who settled in Northern Ireland during the early seventeenth century were of a different race and civilization as well – this meant major differences of mentality and outlook.

2. We cannot, of course, guess what your personal opinion is here, but perhaps these few remarks will help: Certainly there is no easy and simple solution to the problem. A solution is only possible if both sides are willing to make concessions and compromise. Neither side will be able to see all its demands realized; both sides will have to give as well as take.
If you are very interested in this subject, the paperback by Kevin Boyle and Tom Hadden (quoted on page 80) outlines one possible solution to the Ulster problem.

3. She says they are much concerned about getting on with everyday living. They try to make programmes about issues that concern and interest local people, whether Protestant or Catholic.

4. The main similarity is, of course, that they are both divided cities. Views differ about the status of the two cities according to which side of the divide you are on. There are also shootings and killings in both cities. And basically the inhabitants of the two cities are far more concerned about living as normal a life as possible than about anything else.

5. We feel sure you have a number of ideas on this subject. Here are just two points we should like to make: Perhaps this would have meant a more balanced consideration of both the Protestant and Catholic viewpoints, which in turn might have contributed to a fairer handling of England's Irish neighbours. Perhaps the Troubles would never have escalated in the way they have done.
Again, it might have meant that in later centuries Britain's alliances on the Continent would have been different, which would certainly have altered many aspects of European history.

6. People are of course worried that the new buildings may indeed provide better living conditions but be architecturally so ordinary and uninteresting that the town loses its character. However, in recent years, there has been a real effort to restore a number of the older buildings.

7. Specifically the banner was saying "No" to the Anglo-Irish agreement on the future of Northern Ireland, which was signed on November 15th, 1985. This was signed by the Governments of Ireland and of the United Kingdom and grants some say in Northern Irish affairs to the Irish Government in Dublin.

8. Well, the British and the Irish may be different in race, religion and civilization, as we have already pointed out, but in many ways they are nevertheless not all that different. Over the centuries people have been moving in both directions to Britain from Ireland and vice versa. This means that in fact the two peoples have a lot in common as well.

Exercises

1. a) It is very difficult to work and study at the same time.
   b) It takes more than 19 hours a week to do an Open University course thoroughly.
   c) It is very important to talk over doing the course with your family.
   d) It is at the back of all our minds that we could lose our jobs.
   e) It is our job at *The Guardian* to give them as much fact to base their opinions on as possible.

2. a) There are   b) it's   c) There's   d) there's, is there   e) It's, there's   f) There's   g) There's   h) It's   i) It's   j) it's

3. a) law-abiding   b) up to date   c) supporter   d) non-sectarian or non-denominational   e) war or warfare   f) post-graduate

Unit 35

Here are some suggestions on how to answer the **questions**.

1. Naturally we cannot answer this question for you. Certainly any settlement that stands even a small chance of success will have to be carefully balanced and will have to recognize that each community has a definite identity and commitments. We have already pointed out that there can be no winning side (see the answer to question 2 in unit 34).

2. Because the Protestants and Catholics generally live in different parts of town and never mix socially, because the children go to separate schools and then return to their separate areas, where they also spend their free time.

3. Again we cannot answer this question for you. However, it is surely surprising that, in view of the centuries of conflict in Ulster, so many parents from both sides approve of the idea of integrated schooling. It seems to show that the parents think there is little they can do to alter the situation now, but, by giving their children the chance of being educated together, they might be able to change things in the future.

4. Well, for instance, that the children were obviously afraid; that they too were being drawn into the conflict and not just their parents; that because the situation was far more tense there was a greater tendency to keep apart and not mix.

5. For example, that a lot of the holiday groups wanted to keep in contact and therefore came to the HPW club; that some of the children, when they got older, worked as volunteers for HPW (for instance, as escorts with the holiday groups); that practically every family in the Londonderry area must know at least one person who had been away on one of the HPW holidays or workcamps.

6. Corrymeela provides a place where people from both sides can meet, and HPW concentrates on getting the children away from it all for a time and on reaching the parents through the children.
   Hazelwood College, like other integrated schools in Ulster, is a place where children come together to be educated and to share their cultures and attitudes. The parents, too, have an important role to play in the school.
   All three initiatives are putting deeds before words!

7. Here are some examples (there are others of course):
   – He emphasizes how he approves of Prohibition by mentioning how he regards water as a beautiful drink (almost like gin!).
   – Murder is becoming almost unknown, e.g. not a friend of his had been murdered the summer before (but that was certainly very unusual also before Prohibition).
   – His remarks about lager beer and hot toddy rather suggest that he does in fact miss them.
   – He improves his mind by reading a good book of statistics! In that way of course he really does put conversation "where it ought to be", because there would be no friendly and light-hearted conversation if it were on the subject of statistics!
   – He and his friends would not like to return to the old and would vote "by two hundred per cent" to return to Prohibition.
   – His description of the plain room which should be a substitute for the bar is hardly attractive. As if anyone would want to stay in such a room until 2 o'clock in the morning!
   – Under the Prohibition laws alcohol could only be sold if used "for medicinal purposes". Leacock's description of his medicinal use of whiskey in a friend's case tells us a lot about what he thinks of these laws.

Exercises

1. a) Jerry told Linda that just generally it was an issue about even what you called the city.
   b) I'm afraid some people think the situation is hopeless.
   c) Jerry added that he had had no connection with Northern Ireland.
   d) We have always maintained that we see this work (or "that work" if you're talking at a distance) with the youth club as being vital.
   e) She asked Mr McKay where the word "whiskey" actually came from.
   f) Werner Heubeck promised them he would (he'd) show them the sights of Belfast. (You can also say: "...promised to show them the sights of Belfast.)
   g) He says he thinks that's enough for today.

b) Diese Siliziumscheibe besteht aus vielen Reihen kleiner, einzelner, integrierter Schaltungen, den sogenannten Chips. Die Leitungen der einzelnen Schaltungen (Schaltkreise) sind viel zu klein, als daß wir sie mit dem bloßen Auge sehen könnten. Deshalb benutzen die Designer (Planer) diesen Computer, um die Leitungen der einzelnen Schaltungen etwa auf das 250fache zu vergrößern, damit sie sie genau dorthin plazieren (legen) können, wo sie sie hinhaben wollen, um die richtigen Verbindungen innerhalb der Schaltung herstellen zu können. Denn nur so kann die Schaltung natürlich richtig funktionieren. Danach geschieht folgendes: Sie (= die Planer) vollenden ihren Entwurf für die ganze Schaltung und übertragen ihn auf ein Magnetband. Dieses Magnetband geht an die Produktionsabteilung. Die Leute in der Produktion benutzen das Magnetband, um die einzelnen Siliziumscheiben und auf diesen Scheiben die einzelnen Schaltungen herzustellen, wie wir hier sehen können.

Unit 37

Here are some suggestions on how to answer the **questions**.

1. Edinburgh is called the Athens of the North because, like Athens in Greece, it is beautifully situated on and among hills by the sea. There are a number of buildings in Edinburgh which are copies of Greek buildings. And Edinburgh is an important cultural centre – again like Athens in its glorious past.

2. Businessmen go to Edinburgh because it is an important financial centre. Tourists go there because it is a beautiful city. Artists, e.g. actors and musicians, go there for the Festival of Music and Drama, and so do people from all over the world who are fond of the theatre, the opera, the ballet, or concerts.

3. Of course, you all know that Nelson was a famous British admiral. He defeated the French and the Spanish in the sea battle of Trafalgar, in 1805. He died in that battle, but his victory made Britain the most powerful nation on the Seven Seas for as long as one hundred years.

4. In the late 18th and early 19th centuries, almost all European countries showed a deep interest in ancient Greek culture. During that period a lot of copies of Greek temples and monuments were built in Germany, too. Many of them can be found in Berlin and in Bavaria, especially in Munich.

5. No place in Britain is more than eighty miles from the coast. So even families who cannot afford long journeys can enjoy their summer holidays by the sea – even if they only have a day or a weekend to spare.

6. In fine weather people can do a lot of things by the sea, like swimming, sun-bathing, jogging, and playing all kinds of ball games. The children will be happy to build sandcastles or to hunt for pebbles and seashells. But what can they do if the weather is bad? They want a least some entertainment – and things to keep their children happy.

7. British and German seaside resorts have a few things in common: In the summer they are crowded, and in both countries a lot is being offered for entertainment. But you will find less people in German seaside resorts who only come for a day or two, because for most Germans the distance from their home towns to the sea is far too long for that. And there are no pleasure piers, and you will hardly find as many Bingo halls und fish and chips shops as in Britain.

Exercises

1. "Are you American?"
   "No, I'm definitely not American."
   ––
   "Oh, I'm just taking a little vacation, I'm visiting my family. And what are you doing here?"
   ––
   "So you are doing research for school (I see)."
   ––
   "... And have you also heard of Robin Hood? O.K., I will tell you the story."
   ––
   "Tell me, have you ever been to Whitby?"
   "No, I haven't been to Whitby yet."

2. "How about going down to the beach today?" – "Good idea!" – "What time?" – "Eleven o'clock." – "(That's a) bit late! How about ten?" – "Sorry, but I'd like to finish these letters first." – "All right, eleven (o'clock) then!"

3. Linda's report:
"My tour of Edinburgh first took me to a park. Here I met Allan Porteous, an artist and teacher, who was sketching what looked like a small Greek temple: St Bernard's Well. He showed me some more sketches he had done of the city and its surroundings. Some of them showed buildings and monuments on Calton Hill. There were also sketches of streets in Edinburgh and of places just outside the city. At the end of this 'sightseeing tour' I told Allan that it was marvellous and that it was what I would call a quick tour of a town. He replied that we had really just only scratched the surface and that I had to go and look at the things. I said that I wanted to do it straight away, and he offered to show me round. He added that that would cost me a drink. I thought that was typically Scottish, to which he replied, what else did I expect in Scotland?
So we visited all the places I had first seen in Allan's sketchbook. Afterwards I wanted to buy something typically Scottish. I went to a store where they sell pullovers. When I met Allan again at the pub, I could not buy him a drink because I was broke, having spent all my money on woollens. So Allan decided that the drinks would be on him."

Unit 38

Here are some suggestions on how to answer the **questions**.

1. Ireland always stayed Roman Catholic. Many Irish left their country and came to England for work, especially in the 19th century. They brought their religion with them. So did Italian and Spanish workers, who went e.g. to South Wales, looking for jobs in the coal mines. There were also a number of converts – people who decided to become Catholics as grown-up persons. Cardinal John Henry Newman and the author Graham Greene are among those converts.

2. Among the many places of historical interest or natural beauty which are kept up by English Heritage or the National Trust are Dover Castle (unit 27), the Tower of London (unit 28), and the Giant's Causeway (unit 35).

3. In the Federal Republic of Germany, buildings of historical interest and places of natural beauty are looked after by the state (federal, country or town authorities). Only in cases when the authorities show no interest in keeping up a certain building, a park or garden, private persons who care about these buildings or places form a group and raise money in order to keep them in good shape.

4. One has only to look at Britain's coastline and compare it to the coastline of Germany, for example, in order to understand why Britain is one of Europe's most important fishing nations.

5. As in most other trades, machines and other technical devices have been introduced in agriculture and the fishing industry. Fishermen use bigger and faster ships and have a lot of machinery on board. So less people can get more work done.
The other reason for the comparatively small number of fishermen is, of course, that the numbers of fish have been declining.

6. Britain's fishing industry benefits from Britain's membership in the EEC in two ways: (1) the export of fish to other EEC countries is no longer a problem; (2) EEC regulations protect Britain's 12-mile limit; EEC controls also ensure that no country catches more fish than allowed. (If all countries were allowed to catch as many fish as they like, there would not be many fish left in the sea in a couple of years.)

7. The cause for the changes in the number of the various livestock in the U.K. is due to the country's membership of the EEC. There are a number of EEC countries which raise more cattle and calves than they need for their own home markets; so they are not interested in imports from the U.K. On the other hand, there is still a market for sheep, lambs, and wool in other EEC countries.

8. There are at least three reasons why the production per hectare has been increased: (1) the introduction of modern machinery; (2) the introduction of plants which give better results, thanks to agricultural research; (3) the use of chemical fertilizers.

9. Norman's farm is fairly small. He does mixed farming: livestock (mostly sheep) *and* crops.
John's farm is large. He concentrates on a few crops only (potatoes, oilseed). That allows him to equip the farm with all the things needed to produce effectively and economically (potato harvester, large storerooms with air tunnels, conveyer belts). The only question is what this kind of industrialized

agriculture, which includes the use of chemicals and using the soil to grow the same kind of crops again and again, will do to the environment.

10. In October, when all potato crops have been harvested and most farmers put their potatoes on the market, the prices are low. From December to June/July, when no fresh crops are brought to the market, the demand for potatoes is high and the prices go up accordingly.

Exercises

1. (1) regular verb – (2) to form a question – (3) question – (4) question – regular verb – regular verb – (5) "empty" verb, to stress an action – (6) stress – (7) question – (8) question – (9) negation – question – (10) question – regular verb – (11) stress.

2. (12) Der Papst wollte die Scheidung damals nicht gestatten. (would = *want to*) (13) Man kommt hier herüber und holt sich Steine von der Kirche. Würden Sie so etwas nicht tun? (Wouldn't you do it if you had the chance? = *condition*) (14) Wenn es eines gibt, das mir auffällt, dann sind es die Fischerboote. (We cannot render easily in German, that Joe Green is being *careful* here about what he says of a time long ago.) (15) Ich denke schon (daß das Landleben heute um vieles leichter ist). (*carefulness*: the speaker is not quite sure of his own opinion. – In Germany you will often hear "Ich würde meinen" in cases like that.) (16) Ich würde gerne etwas von Ihrem Hof sehen. Würden Sie mich bitte herumführen? (*Polite* way of asking for something.)

3. Would you help me, please? – Would you show me the way to the castle, please? – I would like (I'd like) to see your new potato harvester. – Would you lend me your bicycle, please? – She would like to hear more about the fishing industry. (Would you tell her ..., please?)
   NOTE! In Britain it is considered most impolite to leave out *please* when asking for something!

4. Linda: Joe Green hat mir gesagt, daß man vor 25 Jahren auf Fischerbooten den Hafen überqueren konnte. Heute scheint es nicht mehr so viele zu geben.
   Arthur: Stimmt. Vor 25 Jahren hatten wir in Whitby eine große Heringsfischer-Flotte. Die Boote kamen in den Sommermonaten von anderen Häfen hierher, vor allem von schottischen Häfen. Und bei Flut konnte man wirklich von einem Boot zum anderen quer durch den Hafen laufen, ohne nasse Füße zu bekommen.
   Aber leider haben die Heringsschwärme inzwischen stark abgenommen, und so lohnt es sich für viele Fischer nicht mehr, hier herunterzukommen.
   Linda: Hat sich die Situation für die Fischer durch den Beitritt Großbritanniens zur EG verschlechtert?
   Arthur: Nein, die Situation hat sich nicht verschlechtert. Im Gegenteil: Wir sind froh, daß wir jetzt im europäischen Raum geregelte Zustände haben.
   Früher hatten wir nur unsere eigenen lokalen Gesetze zum Schutz unserer Fischereiflotte. Durch die jetzt geltenden europäischen Gesetze werden die gesamten Fischbestände der Nordsee geschützt. Die Heringsschwärme nehmen (auf Grund der Einführung von Fangquoten) nicht mehr so stark ab wie früher.
   Linda: Aber man hört viel über die Verschmutzung der Nordsee. Wirkt sich das auf die Fischbestände aus?
   Arthur: Ach, wissen Sie, ich schwimme in der Nordsee, und mir hat es noch nicht geschadet.
   Nein, die Fische sind nicht durch Umweltverschmutzung gefährdet, jedenfalls nicht in diesem Teil der Nordsee.
   Der Grad der Verschmutzung ist wirklich sehr, sehr gering. Das Meer hier ist sehr sauber.

Unit 39

Here are some suggestions on how to answer the **questions**.

What do you remember?

(You may not remember all of this, but let us see how much you do remember!)

1. Ferry: ...

2. Dover: ...

3. Betteshanger Colliery in the "Garden of England" (= Kent):
Talks with Peter Heap, Press Officer of the National Coal Board, and with miners about the situation of the coal industry in Kent and in other parts of the country.

4. Canterbury:
Talks with pupils of King's School.

5. London:
Ride on a boat on the River Thames. John, the skipper, talks about changes which are taking place on the river banks.
Meeting with Albert Jones of Lloyd's Insurance. The famous Square Mile (= City of London) with its international markets.
Antiques market in Portobello Road, explained by Henry Gregory.
Visit to Peter Preston, chief editor of *The Guardian*, and Tony Orford of the Printers' Union. Talks about the British Press.
Holland Park Comprehensive School. Margaret Pringle, headmistress, and Chris May, who teaches English to children from foreign countries.

6. Birmingham:
Tour of the old canals. Andrew Blizzard, librarian, talks about the decay of the old industries.
Visit to police headquarters. Superintendent Jim Arthur explains the modern control room, Superintendent Jim Swingewood shows examples of police work in a multi-racial society.
A game of cricket between an English and a West Indian team.

7. Border Country between England and Wales:
Talks with Sue Haverly, who works for SCAR (Severnside Campaign Against Radiation), and Brian Price, harbourmaster near the Lydney und Berkeley nuclear power stations.
John Morgan, writer and BBC broadcaster, talks about the old Forest of Dean.

8. Wales:
Centre for Alternative Technology near Machynlleth. Tim Brown, Press and Public Relations Officer of the Centre. Dolgellau. Olwyn Lloyd Evans, Welsh-speaking young lady.

9. Northern Ireland, Derry/Londonderry:
Maureen Gallagher from Radio Foyle, a BBC local radio station. Club of Holiday Projects West. Jerry Tyrrel, an Englishman who decided to stay in Derry.

10. Belfast:
Frances Kennedy, who grew up in the city, but works as a teacher in Germany now. Werner Heubeck, Managing Director of Ulster Bus, a German who wants to stay in Northern Ireland.

11. The Giant's Causeway and Old Bushmills Distillery on the north coast of Northern Ireland.

12. Stirling:
The Open University's summer school on the university campus. Joe McBride and Cathy Hickman, students of the Open University.
Wendy Faulkner, of SEF (Scottish Enterprise Foundation), explains about Graduate Enterprise and Silicon Glen.
Emma Shipton, a graduate who started her own business in stained glass.

13. Glasgow:
David Shuttleton, another graduate; he makes and repairs Mackintosh furniture. The Willow Tea Room from the 1880s.

14. Livingston, the capital of Silicon Glen:
David Wood, director of an American hi-tech firm in Scotland.

15. Edinburgh:
Allan Porteous, an artist and teacher from the city, introduces Linda to the "Athens of the North".

16. Robin Hood's Bay near Whitby:
First meeting with Joe Green, who now lives in the USA, but returned to his home country for his holidays.

17. Whitby:
    Joe Green explains about the Abbey.
    Arthur Coulson, a fish auctioneer, tells Linda about the situation of the fishing industry in the U.K. Whitby Golf Club.

18. Two Yorkshire farmers:
    Norman Stockdale, who does traditional mixed farming, and John Marsay, whose farm is more of an agricultural factory.

What borders do you remember?

Borders between countries: England/Wales, the Republic of Ireland/Northern Ireland (where Maureen Gallagher's passport was controlled!), Scotland/England (Gretna Green, where more than 10,000 marriages took place).

Time borders: The famous Square Mile of the City of London is almost identical with the ancient Roman Town. – On the banks of the River Thames there are old warehouses next to modern office buildings. – There are the old dying industries (e.g. in Birmingham) and the modern electronic industry (e.g. in Silicon Glen).

Cultural borders: They were most clearly to be seen in Birmingham, but also e.g. at Holland Park Comprehensive School.

Language borders: They are most evident at the Welsh border with its sign-post saying "Croeso i Gymru". But there are a lot of minor ones all over the country: Scottish people have a pronunciation which is clearly different from the English one, and the (Northern) Irish have their own accent as well. Even within England there are different accents, as we could hear listening to John, the skipper (London), Joe McBride (Midlands) or Norman Stockdale (Yorkshire).

Where would you like to go?

This, of course, is a very personal question. We cannot suggest a general answer here. We can only hope that, one day, you will decide to visit the United Kingdom yourself – and that you will enjoy it as much as Linda did.

Wordlist

A

A-level (Advanced Level) (*etwa*) Abiturniveau
abbey Abtei
abbreviate verkürzen
absence Abwesenheit
abuse (n) Beschimpfung
abuse (v) beschimpfen
access Zutritt
according to gemäß, entsprechend
account (n) Bericht, Darstellung
achieve vollbringen, zustande bringen, erreichen
achievement Leistung, Tat
acre Morgen (*Flächenmaß*)
admiration Bewunderung
adolescence Jugend(-zeit, -jahre)
adult erwachsen
adumbration flüchtiger Entwurf, Andeutung
advisory beratend
affiliation Zugehörigkeit
afford sich leisten, sich erlauben
agricultural community Landwirtschaft(swesen)
aim to beabsichtigen, vorhaben
albeit obgleich, wenn auch
amount to sich belaufen auf
ancestor Vorfahre
ancient uralt
apoplexy Schlaganfall
apply for beauftragen
appointment Verabredung, Termin
apposite treffend
appreciate (hoch) schätzen
apt geschickt in, begabt für
aquatic environment Meeresumwelt
arouse erregen
Art Nouveau Jugendstil
assembly Versammlung
asset Vorteil
assurance Zusicherung
at one stage zu einem (früheren) Zeitpunkt
attempt (v) versuchen
augment vermehren, sich steigern
average gross weekly earnings wöchentlicher Durchschnittsbruttoverdienst
aye /*Dialekt*) ja

B

baleful unheilvoll, böse
bane Verhängnis, Verderben
banner Spruchband
barley Gerste
barrier Schleusen
basically prinzipiell, grundsätzlich
batsman Schläger, Schlagmann
be bound to (bestimmt tun) müssen
beacon Leuchtfeuer
beneficiary Nutznießer
benefit from profitieren von
betray verraten
bias Voreingenommenheit
bile Galle; schlechte Laune
bitch (*als Schimpfwort*) Weibsstück, Hure
blame on die Schuld geben, zuschreiben
bleak freudlos, trüb, traurig
blinkered mit Scheuklappen versehen
blow up vergrößern
boarding school Internat
boorish flegelhaft
boost unterstützen, neuen Aufschwung bringen
bounds Grenzen
bowler hat Melone
bows Bug
brass Messing
breather Verschnaufpause, Atempause
bridge (Schiffs-)Brücke
broke pleite
bunch Haufen, Bande
bypass (v) umgehen

C

cancer Krebs
cap-lamp (*sinngemäß*) am Grubenhelm befestigte Lampe
car ferry Autofähre
cardboard box Pappkarton, -schachtel
cardigan Wolljacke
carry out durchführen, erfüllen
carving Schnitzerei, Schnitzwerk
cask Faß
cattle Vieh
causeway erhöhter Weg, Damm
Celt Kelte
change Klein-, Wechselgeld
chat (v) plaudern
childless kinderlos
chuck hinschmeißen
citizen Bürger
claim (v) beanspruchen
clasp (n) Klammer
clear out ausräumen
clergyman Geistlicher
cliff Klippe, Felsen
closure Schließung
cluster (n) Anhäufung
coal stocks Kohlevorräte
coal store Kohlelager
coalfield Kohlengebiet, -revier
coastline Küste(nlinie)
colliery Kohlenbergwerk, Grube, Zeche
come to a head sich zuspitzen
commit to anvertrauen
commute pendeln
compete with konkurrieren mit
competition Wettbewerb
comprehensible verständlich, begreiflich
concern (n) Interesse
conflagration Feuersbrunst
conflict Widerspruch, Streit
connect verbinden
conquer erobern, besiegen
conquest Eroberung
conscience Gewissen
conscious decision bewußte Entscheidung
console (n) Konsole
constable Polizist, Schutzmann
construct errichten
contend behaupten
contract (v) sich zuziehen
contribute beitragen
controversy Streitpunkt, Streitfrage, Kontroverse
convert (v) umbauen
core Kern
correspondence course Fernunterricht
corrupt bestechlich, käuflich, korrupt

coterminous dasselbe Gebiet deckend
countryside Land (*im Gegensatz zur Stadt*)
county Grafschaft
coverage Berichterstattung
crane Kranich
crazy golf Minigolf
crumble away verfallen
curriculum Lehrplan

D

dagger Dolch
damage (n) Schaden
decimate dezimieren
decline (v) abnehmen, zurückgehen
dedication Hingabe
deduct abziehen
Defender of the Faith Verteidiger des Glaubens
deficit Defizit, Mangel
deleterious schädlich, nachteilig
denomination konfessionell, Bekenntnis-
dependable verläßlich
deposit (n) Guthaben, Einzahlung
derelict zerfallen
design (v) gestalten, entwerfen
destiny Schicksal
destruction Zerstörung
deter abschrecken, zurückhalten
devastate verwüsten, zerstören
develop entwickeln; sich (eine Krankheit) zuziehen
device Vorrichtung, Gerät
devoted to gewidmet
dignity Würde
disgrace Schande
display zeigen, zur Schau stellen
distillery Brennerei
distribute ver-, austeilen
diverse verschieden
Dovorian Einwohner Dovers
downtown (Stadt-)Zentrum
drain (v) trockenlegen, entwässern, ableiten
drawbridge Zugbrücke

E

editor-in-chief Chefredakteur
EEC (European Economic Community) E.W.G.
eel Aal

electricity grid Stromnetz
elitist elitär
emerge auftauchen, hochkommen
emergence Auftauchen, Hervorkommen
emphasis Nachdruck
emulate nacheifern
enrol registrieren
enterprise Unternehmen
environment Umwelt
environmentalist Umweltschützer
equip ausrüsten, ausstatten
escalation Eskalation
escort (n) Begleiter(in)
establishment Einrichtung
estuary Mündungsbecken
ethos Ethos
every facet of jede Seite von
evidence Beweismittel
excess überschüssig
excessive übermäßig
exhaust erschöpfen
exhilarate erheitern, aufheitern
exhilarated heiter, angeregt
expanse Ausdehnung
expenditure (finanzielle) Ausgabe
explode umwerfen, zunichte machen, (Illusion) zerstören
exploit ausnützen, ausbeuten
extol preisen, rühmen
extramural department (*etwa*) VHS-Abteilung einer Universität
extrovert (n) Extravertierte(r)

F

faith Glaube(n)
fall flat on one's face Schiffbruch erleiden
fall on hard times schwere Zeiten erleben
fallout Niederschlag, Ausschüttung
fashionable modisch gekleidet, elegant, vornehm
fence (v) fechten
fertilizer Düngemittel
fit (v) into 'reinkriegen, hineinpassen
fleece Vlies, Schaffell
floating schwimmend
flock (v) zuströmen
flood Überschwemmung
focus (v) sich konzentrieren auf
follow-up work (*etwa*) Nacharbeit

fool someone jdm. hereinlegen
for a song für ein Butterbrot, spottbillig
fort Fort, Schanze
fortification Befestigung
fortify befestigen
fortress Festung
fracture (v) brechen
framework Bau(werk)
freesheet Gratisblatt
fuel Brennstoff
fume (n) (gefährlicher) Rauch, Abgas
fund (v) finanzieren, subventionieren
funfair Rummelplatz

G

galley Galeere
garrison Garnison
get hot zu heiß werden (*Boden*)
getaway Zufluchtsort, Versteck
glen Berg-, Felsschlucht
go down hinuntergehen, nachlassen
go on stattfinden, geschehen
go through a bad patch eine Pechsträhne haben
go up emporwachsen, gebaut werden
gothic gotisch
gradually nach und nach, allmählich
graduate (n) Absolvent
graduate (v) absolvieren, graduieren
grammar school (*etwa*) Gymnasium
gratifying erfreulich
gross domestic product Bruttoinlandseinkommen
gross Gros (= 12 Dutzend)
grow up sich entwickeln

H

hack (n) Taxi
hack (v) zerhacken
hackman Taxifahrer
hamlet Weiler, Dörfchen
haunt (v) spuken, heimsuchen
haven Zufluchtsort, Asyl
hawk Habicht
head for zusteuern, Kurs nehmen auf
headmistress Schuldirektorin

heal heilen, gesund machen
heart on sleeve Herz auf der Zunge
hectare Hektar
hemp Hanf
heritage Erbe, Erbschaft
high technology Spitzentechnologie
high-cost mining capacity kostenträchtige Grubenkapazität
highlight (v) hervorheben, herausstellen
hilarity Heiterkeit
hot toddy Grog
Huguenot Hugenotte
husband (v) haushalten mit, sparsam umgehen mit

I

idle faul, träge, nutzlos
ignore keine Beachtung schenken, außer acht lassen
import duty Einfuhrzoll
impossible unmöglich, unglaublich
in the first place zuerst, anfangs
increase steigern, erhöhen
independent nicht staatlich
indication Hinweis
inextricably unentwirrbar
ingredient Bestandteil, Zutat
inherit erben
installation Installation
insulate isolieren
insure versichern
intact unbeschädigt, ganz, intakt
intake Aufnahme
integrated integriert, Einheits-
interfere *hier:* Radio- bzw. Fernsehsendungen stören
intermittent zeitweilig
interrupt unterbrechen
into the bargain obendrein, zusätzlich
investigation Untersuchung
involved in verbunden sein mit
issue (n) Thema, Angelegenheit
issue Streitpunkt
item Gegenstand

J

jangle (v) irritieren

K

keep one's edge im Vorteil bleiben, jdm. gegenüber ein Plus haben
keep pace with Schritt halten mit
keep (n) Bergfried
kill two birds with one stone zwei Fliegen mit einer Klappe schlagen

L

laborious mühsam, anstrengend
lad Junge, Bursche
landmark Wahrzeichen
landscape Landschaft
lark (n) Spaß, Ulk, Vergnügen
lava Lava
law-abiding gesetzestreu
leader Leitartikel
leaflet Flugblatt, Faltblatt
leaning Neigung, Tendenz
leisure Freizeit
leukaemia Leukämie
lifeblood Herzblut
lighthouse Leuchtturm
liken to vergleichen mit
limpid hell, durchsichtig, klar
linen Leinen
liquor starke alkoholische Flüssigkeit, Alkohol
livestock lebendes Inventar, Vieh(bestand)
loads of eine Menge von
look after sich kümmern um
lore and legend (*etwa*) Überlieferung und Legende
low density of workers niedrige Beschäftigtenzahl (z.B. bezogen auf ein bestimmtes Gebiet)
loyal loyal, treu
lunatic asylum Irrenanstalt

M

make allowances for berücksichtigen, bedenken
malt Malz
manage schaffen, zuwege bringen
managing director geschäftsführendes Vorstandsmitglied
mania Manie, Sucht
manual manuell, Hand-
manufactured (extra) schaffen, „fabrizieren"
mature (v) reifen (lassen)

meadow Wiese
mild mild
mill (Textil)Fabrik
mingle sich vermischen
mistake for verwechseln mit
mixed marriage Mischehe
moderate mäßig
monitor (v) überwachen
moonlight (v) Nebenbeschäftigung nachgehen
move in einziehen
multiple chain stores Kettenläden, Einkaufsketten

N

national anthem Nationalhymne
news Nachrichten
newsprint Zeitungspapier
newsvendor Zeitungsverkäufer
nimble flink
non-sectarian nicht konfessionell
nuclear nuklear, Kern-
nutmeg Muskatnuß

O

offender Übeltäter, Missetäter
on a large scale basis in großem Umfang, auf breiterer Basis
oral history mündliche, „lebendige" Geschichte, Zeugenaussage
orchard Obstgarten
outdo übertreffen
outing Ausflug
outperform übertreffen
outset Anfang, Beginn, Aufbruch
overriding allerwichtigste(r), allentscheidende(r)

P

packed überfüllt, dicht zusammengedrängt
panel (Instrumenten)Tafel
pebble Kieselstein
peel (n) Schale, Rinde
peer, peeress Adlige(r)
pelt (v) bewerfen, beschießen
periodical Zeitschrift
persistent beharrlich, hartnäckig
pest Schädling
pickpocket Taschendieb

plant (n) Fabrik
poll Meinungsumfrage
pollute verunreinigen
pollution Verunreinigung
posh vornehm, fein
poultry Federvieh, Geflügel
predictable voraussagbar
prejudice Vorurteil
preliminary einleitend, Vor-
preserve (v) bewahren, schützen
press officer Pressesprecher
pressure Druck, Spannung
prestigious angesehen, hochgeschätzt
pretend vortäuschen, so tun, als ob
previous vorhergehend, voraus-
Principal Schuldirektor, Rektor
principal wichtigst, bedeutendst, Haupt-
professional den freien Berufen zugehörend, Akademiker
prolific fruchtbar
proper richtig, ordentlich
proposition Vorschlag, Anregung
proprietor Eigentümer, Besitzer
prosper gedeihen, blühen
provide besorgen, beschaffen
provide an entree Zugang verschaffen
prowl herumschleichen; durchstreifen
publican Gastwirt
purport (n) Sinn, Bedeutung
purpose Ziel, Zweck

Q

qualify for a grant für einen Zuschuß qualifizieren
quarry Steinbruch
quit aufgeben

R

radiation Strahlung
rail link Bahnverbindung
raise heraufsetzen, steigern
rape Raps
rate of extraction Gewinnungsrate, -geschwindigkeit
rate (n) (Verhältnis)Ziffer, Quote

recital Konzert (Instrumentalmusik oder Gesang)
recreation Erholung, (erholende) Freizeitgestaltung
redevelopment Sanierung (eines Stadtviertels)
reduce verringern, vermindern
reduce costs Kosten reduzieren
refer verweisen
reimburse zurückzahlen
relate to verbinden mit
reliable zuverlässig
remote entlegen
renewable erneuerbar
represent darstellen
research Forschung
resemblance Ähnlichkeit
reserves Vorräte
resort (n) Ferien-, Ausflugsort
responsibility Verantwortung
restrained zurückhaltend, maßvoll
retreat sich zurückziehen, zurückweichen
revenue Einkommen
ride the shaft in den Schacht fahren
ridge Kamm, Grat
riot (n) Tumult, Auflauf
risk Risiko
road link Straßenverbindung
rock Zuckerstange (Spezialität der britischen Seeorte)
ruin Ruine
rural ländlich

S

safeguard schützen, sichern
safety hook Sicherheitshaken
scales Waage
score (v) (einen Treffer) erzielen
scrape (v) kratzen, schaben
scratch (v) kratzen, ritzen
screen (n) Bildschirm
seashell Seemuschel
secondary modern school (etwa) Realschule
security Sicherheitsbereich
sempstress, seamstress Näherin
serviced to meet the demands mit allen notwendigen Dienstleistungen ausgestattet

settle sich niederlassen
setup Aufbau, Organisation
shape Zustand
share (n) Anteil
shipping operator Schiffsfahrtunternehmer, Reeder(ei)
shoal, school (Fisch-)Schwarm
siege (n) Belagerung
sights Sehenswürdigkeiten
significance Bedeutung
silicon Silizium
silver-plated versilbert
site Gelände
sizeable umfangreich, beträchtlich
skilled gelernt, fachlich ausgebildet
slogan Schlachtwort, Slogan
slot machine Automat
soil Erde, Boden
solar panel Solarmodul, -paneel
solidity Festigkeit
soul-searching Gewissenserforschung
source Quelle
spectator Zuschauer
spiky spitz
spire Kirchturm(spitze)
sports results Sportergebnisse
sprawl sich (unregelmäßig) ausdehnen
spring up aus der Erde schießen
squalid schmutzig, verwahrlost, verkommen
stained glass Glasgemälde, Produkt der Glasmalerei
stalwart Unentwegte(r), treuer Anhänger
stitch (n) (Seiten)Stechen
stock Bestand
stocks and shares Aktien
strain (n) Spannung
strap (v) festschnallen
strife Streit, Zank
structure Bau, Gebäude
stuff Zeug
subject Untertan
subsidy Subvention
successor Nachfolger
sufficient genügend, ausreichend
supply (v) liefern, versorgen
support (n) Unterstützung
supporter Anhänger
survive überleben, überdauern
swallow up verschlingen, aufnehmen

T

tabloid Sensationsblatt, Bildzeitung
take apart auseinandernehmen
tattoo Zapfenstreich
taunt (v) spotten, verhöhnen
technology Technologie
temper (v) härten
term Trimester, Quartal
terraced house Reihenhaus
thatched roof Strohdach
the die is cast die Würfel sind gefallen
the great divide die große Trennlinie
this is on me das bezahle ich; dies geht auf meine Kosten
thrive gedeihen
thriving gedeihend, blühend
tidal Gezeiten-, den Gezeiten unterworfen
tide Gezeiten
tidy sauber, ordentlich
tireless unermüdlich
title Druckschrift
tombstone Grabstein
tongue in cheek ironisch
tonne (metrische) Tonne
torment (v) peinigen, foltern
traded market price gehandelter Marktpreis
trading Handel
traffic level Verkehrsaufkommen
transact durchführen
transform into umwandeln in
treatment Behandlung
tripartite dreiteilig
Troubles Unruhen
trust (n) Treuhandgesellschaft, Stiftung
tube Röhre
tumbler Trinkglas, Becher
turn a blind eye ein Auge zudrücken

U

uncommitted ungebunden
underfunded unterfinanziert, mit zu wenig Mitteln ausgestattet
unite vereinigen, etwas geschlossen tun
unrelieved ungelindert, ungemildert
unrestrained ungehemmt, zügellos
untapped unerschlossen
update neuester Stand
uprising Aufstand
urban man Städter
urban redevelopment Stadtsanierung
urban städtisch

V

vessel Schiff
vexatious lästig, störend
viable lebensfähig
vice versa umgekehrt
vicinity Nachbarschaft, Nähe
vicious circle Teufelskreis
vicious bösartig, boshaft
vineyard Weinberg
virtual faktisch
volunteer (n) Freiwillige(r)

W

wade in sich hineinstürzen
wafer Mikroplättchen, Scheibchen
warehouse Lagerhaus
warfare Kriegsführung
waste (n) Abfall
watercress Brunnenkresse
weaving Webkunst
wee (*Dialekt*) klein
welcome (v) aboard willkommen an Bord heißen
wharf Kai
wheelhouse Steuerhaus
wild life Tiere in freier Wildbahn
winding sich windend, schlängelnd
with no strings attached ohne Bedingungen
withdrawal Herausnahme (aus einer Schulklasse)
woollens Wollwaren, Strickwaren
working relationship Arbeitsverhältnis
worn-out abgetragen, überholt
worthwhile der Mühe wert

Y

yeast Hefe
yobbish unerzogen und rowdyhaft